PRAISE FOR
The Decisive Manag

T0015533

"Barbara Mitchell and Cornelia Gamlem know that the key to a successful organization is leadership and people. Their new book, *The Decisive Manager*, provides a blueprint for leaders to create an environment where employees feel valued, appreciated, and heard, which can result in increased productivity, profitability, and workforce retention. Not to mention less stress for leaders by knowing these key points to being a Decisive Manager! When it comes to being an effective leader and understanding the importance of decision-making, you can't overlook this thought-provoking book!"
> —**David Asheim, CEO and founder of Engage by Cell**

"*The Decisive Manager* moves beyond the rules of HR into the art of management. Good people stay not just because you pay them well, but also because they have challenging and exciting jobs. They stay because they see a future that lets them grow. Mitchell and Gamlem help you understand this and much more."
> —**Paul Shank, PhD, MBA, retired health care executive and author of *Can Healthcare Get Better?***

"Every manager encounters unexpected people issues that they feel uncomfortable discussing with another manager or HR leader. The Q&A format of this book gets right to answering those questions that many managers face. The authors have captured and addressed so many of these questions and situations in *The Decisive Manager*. Every organization should purchase this book for all levels of management."
> —**Lisa Anderson, SPHR, SHRM-SCP, CPC, chief HR officer at Sev1Tech and author of *Invisible Professional to Influential Leader***

"Managers tend to be decisive with technical issues but often stumble with people issues: Is it okay for me to explain why someone isn't getting a job? Are sign-in bonuses worth it? *The Decisive Manager* is an enjoyable and comprehensive book that provides answers in scenario reality bites. The authors have researched the most useful people "questions and answers" that are evolving in today's workplace and this serves as a powerful resource for managers, professors, students, and practitioners from any industry."
> —**Dr. Virginia Bianco-Mathis, professor and consultant in leadership and management**

THE
DECISIVE
MANAGER

OTHER BOOKS BY THESE AUTHORS

Barbara Mitchell & Cornelia Gamlem:
The Big Book of HR
The Essential Workplace Conflict Handbook
The Conflict Resolution Phrase Book
The Manager's Answer Book
They Did What? Unbelievable Tales from the Workplace

Barbara Mitchell & Sharon Armstrong:
The Essential HR Handbook

If you enjoyed this book, or any of our other books,
we'd be honored if you would post a great review on
Amazon or Goodreads. Mention something that
you really liked about the book(s) and why.
The most impactful reviews are short and succinct.

THE
DECISIVE
MANAGER

Get Results, Build Morale, and
Be the Boss Your People Deserve

Barbara Mitchell

AND

Cornelia Gamlem

This edition first published in 2023 by Career Press, an imprint of
Red Wheel/Weiser, LLC
With offices at:
65 Parker Street, Suite 7
Newburyport, MA 01950
www.careerpress.com
www.redwheelweiser.com

ISBN: 978-1-63265-201-0

Library of Congress Cataloging-in-Publication Data available upon request.

Cover design by Howard Grossman
Interior by Timm Bryson, em em design, LLC
Typeset in Minion Pro

Printed in the United States of America
IBI
10 9 8 7 6 5 4 3 2 1

*To all of the managers
who lead their staff through all types of turbulence,
and the fabulous HR leaders and teams who guide them.*

TABLE OF CONTENTS

ACKNOWLEDGMENTS

During our journey of writing our books, many friends, colleagues, and professionals helped us to bring them to completion and publicize them in the marketplace.

We can never express enough gratitude to some special contributors starting with our literary agent and friend, Marilyn Allen, of the Allen Literary Agency, for her help and advice. You continue to encourage us and advocate for us every step of the way, and you are always there when we need you. All of the things that you've taught us about the publishing industry have been not only insightful, but priceless. Thank you for sharing all of your knowledge and wisdom as we've progressed in this journey.

We cannot forget the booksellers who see the value of our books and display them on the shelves of both brick-and-mortar and virtual stores. We are especially grateful to Cal Hunter who has given our books wonderful exposure by prominently facing and displaying them, and even putting one in the window of Barnes and Noble on Fifth Avenue in New York.

Erik Gamlem has kept our social media efforts on track for many years, always ensuring that everything was up to date. We're grateful for all you have taught us and shared along the way.

Jennifer Seaman was one of our first publicists, and she still provides us with support to this day. You have introduced us to great media sources, many of whom continue to interview us. Thanks for your guidance and your friendship.

A very special thanks to Steve Becker, Steve Becker Publicity, who has arranged some wonderful airtime for us with radio stations and podcasts around the country over the course of this journey. Steve, you are a joy to work with, and we so appreciate all your support.

And to everyone at Career Press, an imprint of Red Wheel/Weiser, we'd like to thank them for their support and their confidence in us. We want to especially acknowledge Eryn Eaton and all the marketing support you provide during our book launches. Your professionalism, dedication, and willingness to help have been amazing.

A special thanks to our families for unconditional love and support always.

Finally, we want to thank and acknowledge you, our readers. Leaders cannot lead without followers. Authors cannot write without readers. We sincerely appreciate all of the support we receive from you.

INTRODUCTION:
HOW TO USE THIS BOOK

People drive success. When you have the right people working for you, they can help your organization achieve growth and thrive. So, it's crucial to treat them right.

This isn't always easy. Most of the issues an organization has are people issues—issues and situations that must be properly and promptly addressed and managed. Doing so is not an easy endeavor.

People issues can be complicated because every person is a unique individual, and there is not necessarily a one-size-fits-all approach that a manager can take. When you add to that all the changes that have occurred in the world of work in recent years—changes to the workplace and the workforce—coupled with the increasing potential for legal risk, all of the complications and challenges are compounded.

If people are the key to success, then organizations need to spend time preparing managers for the most critical part of their job. Unfortunately, and all too often, organizations take their best performing employees or their best technical experts and promote them into management roles without adequately preparing them to lead people. Suddenly, you're a manager. So now what?

The reality is that it can be difficult to anticipate all the issues a manager may face on a day-to-day basis. Even the most experienced managers can be surprised by a new situation, leaving them feeling vulnerable. New and seasoned managers can be overwhelmed by their responsibilities at times. When those responsibilities involve managing your staff, you can't fly by the seat of your pants, take an educated guess, ignore it, or just throw up your hands and give up.

That's where *The Decisive Manager* can help. This book answers questions about every aspect of managing people—from hiring to firing and everything in between. It includes six sections devoted to the following topics. Within each section, there are questions based on situations that managers have actually encountered or can expect to encounter. Since managing people is often complex, there are also questions and answers about issues that you, a manager, may have never thought to ask.

- **Finding and Hiring the Best Talent.** This is such a key component of being a successful manager, but it may be more involved than you think. This section answers questions about recruiting, interviewing, job posting, job offers, onboarding, and more.
- **Creating a Positive Employee Experience.** Once you've identified and hired the right talent, it's important that they want to stay and be productive. If you're wondering how to do this, answers to questions about employee engagement, retention, and motivation are included in this section.
- **Paying and Rewarding Employees.** Pay and benefits are not the only thing that keep employees engaged and motivated, but they are important, especially in today's workplace. Compensation transparency, employee wellness and mental health, and rewards and recognition are just some of the topics that are addressed in this section.
- **Helping Employees Grow and Develop.** You can't expect employees to stay in the jobs they were hired into indefinitely any more than you can expect your organization to remain static. This section answers questions about creating a learning culture, strategies for doing so, and the manager's role in employee development.

- **Understanding Policies and Practices.** Policies, especially those about people and human resource issues, can be daunting. If you wonder about the role policies play in managing, how to apply policies to specific situations, documenting and investigating issues, and employee activism, you'll find answers to these issues and more.
- **Ensuring Graceful Endings.** Employment relationships end under all sorts of circumstances. It's important that they end gracefully and with respect. Some of the questions explored in this section are about layoffs and exit interviews.

Beyond those typical circumstances, what about **Navigating the Changing Workplace**, especially since the pandemic of 2020? There is a subtopic in each section that addresses many of these issues such as mobile technology, hybrid workforces, diversity, and the use of gender pronouns.

Want to **Avoid Legal Pitfalls?** Each section also includes a subtopic devoted to typical situations that could land the uninformed manager in a legal quagmire. Some are questions that managers are likely to wonder about, and others are ones that may come as a surprise.

You may be thinking, wait a minute. Isn't dealing with all the people issues the job of a Human Resources department? Not really. If you are fortunate to work in an organization that has an HR department with a knowedgable staff, they can be a source of valuable information and guidance. They can provide a manager with sound advice and recommendations based on individual circumstance. They are not, however, the ultimate decision maker. You, the manager, are. So it's important that you have some background and working knowledge when you find yourself having to sit down with HR.

Of course, there are many organizations and small business owners who don't have dedicated, internal, HR teams. *The Decisive Manager* is a resource for helping managers help themselves with the people issues they are certain to encounter. If you're looking for a particular topic, you will notice critical terms are in bold font throughout the book, or you can refer to the index.

As you go through this book, you may be thinking:

Question: Where can I find more information about managing people?

Answer: Pick up a copy of *The Big Book of HR*.

Question: What type of information will I find in *The Big Book of HR* that will help me as a manager?

Answer: There are chapters in *The Big Book of HR* devoted to interviewing, hiring, and onboarding as well as the role of the manager. The employee experience is so important, and there are chapters providing insight to employee engagement, employee retention, rewards and recognition, and flexibility. Managers play an integral part in employee development, so you'll be interested in reading about assessing employee development needs and best approaches to meeting them, along with the role of a coach and performance management. Workplace harassment is an important topic, and there is a chapter devoted to it. Finally, throughout the book you will find overviews of relevant employment laws that can help you avoid potential legal pitfalls.

We live in a time when people centricity is so important. You have the most treasured resource in your organization—the human resource. Both *The Decisive Manager* and *The Big Book of HR* are sources for you and anyone who manages people to work effectively with that treasured resource.

SECTION 1

FINDING AND HIRING THE BEST TALENT

THERE IS NOTHING more important than having the right people in the right positions to make your organization a success. It is a challenge to attract and hire the best talent available. Competition is fierce, so how you post open positions; how you treat candidates for positions; and how you make offers can put you at the front of the line for great hires. Now that you've hired them, how do you bring them into your organization's culture?

If you're wondering about offering hiring bonuses, or the secrets to successful video interviews, or the best ways to attract and hire Generation Z, or conducting pre-employment testing, these topics and more are in this section.

Question: After interviewing several candidates for a position, an offer has been prepared for the one considered the best fit for the job. Once the offer is accepted, I want to notify the other candidates, but I'm not sure how to do so. If I send an email, candidates can take their time to read and process the bad news. Is it better to call the candidates so I can deliver the bad news personally and offer feedback if requested?

Answer: Congratulations on doing the right thing and notifying candidates who weren't selected. It is stunning how many organizations skip this step, which is a serious mistake. Whether or not the candidate is the one you want to hire, they have taken their time to interview with your organization, and they deserve to know whether or not they got the job.

It is good to keep in mind that every applicant is a future customer or member for your organization. How you treat them impacts their opinion of your firm and your reputation in the marketplace. Trust us—people tell other people how they are treated in job interviews. You want to maintain your status as a good place to work.

The recommended way to notify the nonselected candidates is to email them with a short but informational message that thanks them for their interest in your organization and for their time spent in interviewing with you. Let them know you think they have a great background but that you have selected an applicant whose experience more closely met your needs. If you mean it, let them know you will retain their resume for possible future openings, but don't make any promises you don't intend to keep.

For example, don't commit to offering them the next available opening. How do you know their skill set will remotely fit the next job you post on social media?

Phone calls can be problematic since they open up the possibility of the candidate pinning you down as to why you didn't hire them, and that is fraught with potential legal issues—so use a well-written email, and end by wishing them success in their search.

Question: At a recent networking event I met someone who I think would be perfect for an upcoming opening in my department. I'd like to bring them in for an interview as soon as possible and get started on the hiring process. However, I'm likely to be told that I have to adhere to a process of recruiting and interviewing several candidates. Why do I have to comply with such an arbitrary process?

Answer: I understand your frustration, but there is a good reason why we recommend you follow an established process when **recruiting and interviewing** potential employees. You want to give every applicant, including the one you recently met, an equal chance of being selected for the position. This means using the same process for everyone so that you won't be accused of favoritism in any way, shape, or form.

Posting jobs externally allows employers to attract a wide and diverse pool of candidates. Your job postings and your jobs or careers page on your website should clearly outline the process your organization uses. For example, you might let applicants know that the first step is for them to submit an application using the form on your website. Then, let them know they will receive acknowledgement that their application has been received (which does not indicate they will be interviewed and/or hired—just that they will be carefully considered). If there is further interest, they will receive an invitation to do a video or phone screening interview. The interview process continues assuming there is mutual interest, until a decision is reached to make an offer or end the process. Before an offer is made, references will be checked.

Follow your established process and your organization will hire qualified staff members and avoid potential legal action.

Question: We've been having a debate in my organization about job offers. Some people say the manager should make the job offer, while others say it should come from human resources so it's consistent. Do you have any thoughts?

Answer: Let's take a look at the pluses and minuses of each approach for making **job offers**. If the manager makes a verbal job offer, it sends a powerful message to the candidate that they are valued. After all, the hiring manager is their future boss.

However, consider the scenario where an employee received a job offer for a regular full-time position from a hiring manager after working as a temporary hire. When the employee received their first paycheck, they realized the salary was much lower than the one offered. The hiring manager admitted he had misquoted the salary and could do nothing to remedy it for six months.

Whoa, this organization had some poor processes in place, which had repercussions. For starters, the employee never received an offer letter nor anything in writing. This carelessness caused them to lose a good employee who took another position for which they interviewed that was still available. Finally, their reputation suffered. While not all managers and organizations are this careless, this is an example of why some organizations have HR make all job offers.

While there's no right answer, there are a number of things to consider, including the size, structure, and nature of your business and industry. You should, however, have a process that documents the terms of the offer, particularly the salary, and get the manager's signature. This provides a record of the intended salary.

If the hiring manager is to be involved, the best practice is to allow them to make the verbal offer, using a script that HR prepared. Follow the verbal offer by a written offer letter from HR. Email the offer letter and then send a hard copy via USPS. HR can follow up on the acceptance process. Of course, be sure you have your legal advisors review your standard offer letter and any other more specific ones, such as for senior leadership.

Question: Is it worth our time to check references? If so, we've been contacted by organizations that will check references for us. It sounds like a good idea and a time saver, but we wonder if it will help us make good hiring decisions. Seems to me that we should do it ourselves, but I have colleagues who don't agree and think we should outsource this part of the hiring process. Any advice about best practices?

Answer: Yes, it is a very good idea to check **references**. You want to confirm what you've heard from the applicant, and if you ask open-ended questions, you may learn a lot from the reference. This can be important information as you make your hiring decision.

A best practice is to have the hiring manager conduct the **reference checks**. HR can help with good questions, but the hiring manager knows the job better than anyone else, and the new hire will be join-ing their team so get them involved in the process.

Another good reason to have the manager conduct reference checks is that many organizations have policies of only verifying employment—confirming an individual was employed, their dates of employment, and the positions they held. A hiring manager may be able to contact the candidate's former supervisor or manager and obtain more detailed information. A hiring manager can also reach out to contacts in their professional networks.

We are also hearing about reference checking services. You're right, they may save you time but carefully check their references before you hire them. Some of them check references online with no follow up. Most of them check references much earlier in the hiring process—sometimes even before an applicant is screened. This sig-nificantly adds to the cost you will pay for something you can easily do yourself.

Question: We've always posted jobs internally as promoting from within is one of our core values. Some employees who interview for a promotion but don't get the job leave the organization. They may have left anyway, but some of our leaders want to stop posting. Is that a good idea?

Answer: Please don't stop your **internal job posting** practice. Here is where you may need to do some research. What may be happening is that certain managers are not doing a good job in communicating the decision about why an internal candidate was not chosen for the position and therefore not promoted.

The decision must be made on the requirements of the open posi-tion and the skills and abilities of the candidates. Once the decision is made, any internal candidate has to be told they didn't get the job and why.

Consider preparing a script for these situations for managers to follow. Include compliments on the employees' skills and their contributions to your organization, but share where they fell short. Give them some encouragement as to what they can do to be better positioned when the next opportunity comes up. Don't, however, make any promises like if you finish your degree, the next one is yours.

It's important to do exit interviews when people leave you. When someone resigns soon after not being selected for a promotion, ask if that contributed to their decision. This information may help you work with your managers to be sure they are not saying the wrong thing.

Today's employees are extremely interested in developing their skills, and if you're not providing enough learning and development opportunities, you may not be able to retain your top performers whether they get promoted or not. So, increase learning opportunities and see if it has an impact on retention. Most likely, it will.

Question: The competition for finding and hiring qualified people is strong. When we have a job opening, we seem to use the tried-and-true job postings we've always used, and we're not getting candidates. Should we be doing something different?

Answer: If you're like most organizations, as soon as a job is open, you pull out the **job description** and post it. This will not work with today's job market and with today's job seekers. You need to think of an **external job posting** as a marketing tool. In fact, if your organization has a marketing department or marketing specialists, sit down with one of them and ask for help. You need to sell your organization as a great place to work and the open position as an opportunity not to be missed. A job description isn't going to make that happen.

Start by thinking like a prospective candidate. As you complete the application, what would you need to know about the organization and the open position? Use those thoughts to help you craft a lively and informative post that lets a potential applicant know about your organization's culture, its leadership, its growth projections, its development opportunities, its mission, and its values. Get the idea?

Use bullet points, short sentences or phrases, and above all, avoid jargon and acronyms. Remember, you want to get people interested in your organization and in the position and not scare them away.

Take some time and look at what your competitors are posting. What are they sharing? What language are they using? We are in a contest for talent, and you want to attract the best that is available. To compete, you need well-written job postings that give the right information in a way that makes the potential applicant move right to the act of completing your application.

Question: What is the appropriate number of interviews before making a job offer? I am reading that today's applicants are unhappy with the number of interviews they endure before getting an offer or being rejected.

Answer: Great question, but you are probably not going to like the answer, which is—it depends, particularly on the nature and level of the position. You're right that applicants do get frustrated with being interviewed multiple times and especially when they are asked the same questions over and over.

However, you do want to get as much information as possible from an applicant, and you do want to get input from colleagues in order to make a good hiring decision. What is the best way to do this?

Start with a 30-minute **screening interview** that either someone from your recruiting staff or the hiring manager conducts by video or phone. This is where you find out if the applicant has the minimum qualifications for the position and is in the right salary range. Follow a script so that each applicant is asked the same questions.

Based on the responses, decide whether to move the applicant forward in the process. If so, consider who you want to join you as you continue the interview process. Select colleagues or others who may interact with the applicant if hired. You can also include someone who will be a peer.

Put together a hiring plan that includes specific questions for each person to ask so that you get a variety of information. While there is no set number of interviews needed to make a good decision, three or four interviews is probably enough when combined with the information you gather during your own interview and then the **reference checks**.

Do your best to have all **in-person interviews** on one day so the applicant's time is maximized. At the end of the day, collect information from your fellow interviewers and decide whether or not the applicant will move forward in the process.

Always let the applicants know what your process is, including how many interviews are possible and your projected decision date. Keeping applicants informed throughout the process will make a huge difference in your ability to hire them.

There is nothing more important than hiring the right people, so do your best to make each interview count.

Question: I've participated in panel interviews in the past. Now, I'm hearing organizations are doing group interviews. I'm not sure what group interviews are, nor how they differ from panel interviews. I'm wondering if my organization should consider conducting group interviews and if there are ways of making panel interviews more effective and successful. Can you enlighten me on these issues?

Answer: Let's start with the **panel interview** where a candidate meets with a hiring manager and some selected peers to spend an hour or so with the applicant. The benefits of a panel interview for the organization include saving time and allowing all the people making the hiring decision to hear all the same information at the same time. They can be effective, but they take some planning so that each panel member has a series of interview questions to ask to avoid the applicant being asked the same question over and over.

This can be accomplished by developing an interview format with scripted questions that each interviewer uses. This also ensures that all applicants are asked the same questions. The interview script can also be used by the hiring manager to collect impressions and information provided by the applicant.

Panel interviews are a bit more difficult for applicants. No longer is the format a conversation between two people—the hiring manager and the applicant. Now, it is a group of people all asking questions of one person, and that can be intimidating. The benefit of a panel interview for the applicant is in the time saved by meeting multiple people at once versus multiple visits or Zoom calls.

Group interviews are primarily used in hospitality or retail organizations where significant numbers need to be hired at the same time—perhaps for seasonal positions. They are just what they sound like—one or more interviewers meet with a group of possible new hires all at once. This saves time and, if structured appropriately, can give the organization valuable information to use in hiring. The key is preparing your questions ahead of time and having the right team in place who can ask questions, listen to responses, observe interaction between applicants, and decide who has strong assessment skills.

Only you can decide which format is possible for your organization or whether the one-on-one interview format is best for you. Good luck.

Question: We are thinking of contacting some former employees to fill many of our openings we have right now. What advice do you have for bringing back good people who left us?

Answer: This is potentially a good idea, but there are some important things to consider before you bring what are commonly called **"boomerang" employees** back to your organization.

Let's start with the positives. Former employees know your culture and were successful while they worked for you. You also know their strengths and weaknesses, so it makes it easy to determine where to place them.

Keep in mind that you should interview them just like any other applicant. You want to learn more about why they left you in the first place and why they would want to come back now. You will also want to learn about what they have been doing since leaving your organization:

- What new knowledge do they have?
- What new experiences have they had?
- Will their new responsibilities be similar to what they did before?
- What will make it work now if it didn't before?

Also, do some probing to find out if:

- Do they have a future focus, or are they stuck in the past?
- Will returning to your organization energize them, or are they looking to come back because it is comfortable?

Before you make the decision to bring back former employees, decide how you will handle the issue of past service credit. This issue can make a big difference if you have benefits that are time bound. For example, will their past service count toward vacation time or **vesting** in your 401(k) programs? Also, don't overlook the **onboarding** process for a rehire, and have them participate in it so they learn what's new and how it impacts them.

Some organizations have found hiring "boomerangs" to be a great way to fill the large number of openings, but you will need to evaluate whether it will work for you and your culture. Don't overlook it as a strategy, but do your research before jumping in with both feet.

Question: We seem to be turned down a lot when we make job offers. We think we do a good job of connecting with candidates and making an offer that they will accept, but we get a lot of rejections. We spend a lot of time and money on recruiting, and it is discouraging to have an offer rejected. What are we doing wrong?

Answer: If it makes you feel any better, it may not be anything you did or didn't do that causes a candidate to reject an offer. It may simply be "it's not you—it's me."

The candidate may have been interviewing with multiple employers and received a better **job offer**; or at the last minute, they decided not to leave their current employer. Likely, there is nothing you could have done differently to be the winner.

However, if you are seeing a pattern of offer rejections, consider reaching out to the candidates and ask what you could have done differently. If you do, don't wait too long after the rejection. You want to get the true story before the candidate forgets.

A better offer can include a higher salary, even if you thought you made a good financial offer; more **flexibility**; more **paid time off** (PTO) or a richer benefits package; or more **employee development opportunities**. If you get that kind of information, don't overlook it. Take time to see if there are things you could improve.

Provide some professional development to anyone who interviews candidates, including top-level management and recruiters. Focus on improving their questioning and listening techniques. You want them to be able to probe for what is really important to any job finalist and use that information to craft an offer that stands the chance of being accepted.

Many candidates turn down an offer because of something that happened during the interview process. Perhaps a recruiter didn't respond as quickly as they wanted to a question or a request. They may have made multiple trips to your office, or Zoom calls, for an interview rather than batching the interviews to cut down time.

Remember, candidates are evaluating your organization all throughout the interview process, and thinking, "If this is the way they treat applicants, what will it be like to work here?" Take the time to analyze your process against the reasons why you get turned down, and do your best to make improvements. Odds are your acceptance rate will improve.

Question: Some of our competitors offer hiring bonuses for hard to fill positions. I don't like the idea of paying someone before they make any kind of contribution to our success. Is this a good idea and if so, how does it work?

Answer: While I understand your hesitancy, there is some merit to this practice. You're absolutely right—**hiring bonuses** are gaining popularity as the pool of available talent shrinks, so you may want to consider adding hiring bonuses to your hiring strategies.

Here are some things to keep in mind as you put your plan together:

- Be selective when announcing bonuses for hard-to-fill jobs. Carefully analyze where you are having the most difficulty finding applicants. Don't make adding a hiring bonus the first thing you try as you are sourcing candidates. Cast a wide net for applicants and use every available resource at your disposal before considering a bonus.
- Before you consider a hiring bonus program, make sure your jobs page on your website is as good as it can be and that your salaries and benefits are as competitive as you can afford. If you're not competitive, a hiring bonus is probably not going to find you the candidates you need.
- Carefully monitor if the bonus brings in quality candidates— people who have the skills you need and who most likely wouldn't have applied otherwise.
- Put a time limit on the bonus program. For example, give it a two-month trial and then take it off your marketing materials and evaluate its effectiveness. If it brought you what you needed, reinstate it with some different parameters to increase attention.

You may find a hiring bonus program works for your organization—at least in the short term. But keep refining your sourcing strategies, including networking, virtual job fairs, LinkedIn, mobile sites, and your organization's website, which often is your most successful source. Good luck.

Question: We monitor the sites where former employees or job applicants can post reviews. Recently, there have been several negative comments about our hiring practices. Is this important, and if so, what should we do?

Answer: **Negative employment reviews** are important at any time, but when most employers are struggling to retain talented employees and/or replace people who leave, monitoring your reviews on Glass Door or other sites is critical.

After checking with your leadership, start by talking with your recruiting team. Are they happy with their jobs and your organization? If the people who have the most interaction with job candidates are not really high on your organization, they may be negatively impacting applicants. If they are not passionate about bringing in the best talent available, odds are you will continue to get poor reviews.

Listen to the **recruiters'** frustrations:

- What is the number of open requisitions each recruiter is tasked with filling, and is it reasonable? Are you spreading them too thin?
- Do they get cooperation from hiring managers when they present a candidate?
- Are they burned out because they are filling the same jobs over and over?
- Are they happy with their compensation? If not, is it possible to provide spot bonuses for filling hard-to-fill positions or granting out-of-cycle salary increases?

Remember that bringing in the best talent is *the* most important thing your organization must do to succeed. It doesn't matter how good your product or service is if you don't have the right team of people to produce or deliver it.

Just as you want your team members to have a positive **employee experience**, you want your applicants to have a stellar **candidate experience**. In today's highly competitive hiring market, time is critical. Good candidates don't remain in the job market for long, so you must move as quickly as possible to interview a talented candidate. If you move too slowly, you may miss out on a superstar who also might be the candidate who posts a negative review. They will have a valid complaint if they were expected to wait a long time between applying and being interviewed by your company.

Question: When we have a job opening, especially in a difficult labor market, my organization immediately looks to fill the job from the outside. I'm thinking we may be overlooking our current workforce. I know promoting a current employee means we have to back fill their position, but do I have a valid point, and if so, how should I approach my supervisor with my idea?

Answer: You raise a great point that frustrates many talented employees who feel they are not considered for openings in their own organization. A policy requiring job openings to be posted internally before they are posted externally can address this frustration. This gives internal candidates the opportunity to let the organization know they feel they are ready for a move and have the skills to take on the new opportunity.

Of course, an **internal job posting** policy must not set any false expectations that internal candidates will automatically be hired. The policy must be clear that internal applicants will be interviewed and their qualifications carefully evaluated before a decision is made.

There are many benefits of promoting from within. The internal applicant:

- Is known to the organization
- Will most likely have a shorter learning time before being productive
- Already knows your culture

The greatest benefit to internal hiring is the morale boost it provides for other employees. A policy of internal job posting prior to going outside the organization is seen as positive by most employees. Your organization is seen as a place where people can get promoted, and they don't have to leave the organization to take a big step in their career.

There are negatives to hiring from within which include:

- You miss the new ideas that would come from hiring from outside the organization.
- You may stir up competition between internal applicants and need to manage expectations.

As for helping you sell this idea to your supervisor, do your research and plan ahead what you plan to say. Set an appointment to discuss this idea so that you will have your supervisor's full attention. Consider putting your idea in writing and sending it ahead of time so your supervisor has a chance to think about it. Stress the positive aspects of an internal posting policy.

You also may want to discuss this with some of your colleagues who can champion your idea.

We wish you good luck.

Question: We are having an internal debate: Is it better to just hire someone we know isn't qualified for the job than to keep a job unfilled while we wait for the perfect candidate? What are your thoughts?

Answer: First of all, there is no perfect candidate for any position, or if there is, they are few and far between. Secondly and much more important, no, it is not better to hire. There is a saying we love, "It is better to hire smart than manage tough."

It is extremely dangerous to fill a job just to fill a job. I once heard this described as the mirror test—holding a mirror under the candidate's nose and if it fogs up, hire them.

Any new hire who joins your organization is going to take effort to bring them up to speed. They are going to impact others on their team. They will impact productivity as their manager will need to devote more effort to their job training.

Then there is the issue of needing to let them go when they just aren't up for the job. There will be **counseling** time and/or **coaching** time. You will need to document where they are falling short. And, if there is a decision to terminate them, there is time to meet with your HR and legal advisors to put all your ducks in a row.

Some might say that this answer is very negative and argue that the new hire might surprise you and do a good job. Yes, that might happen, but experience has shown that this rarely happens. If someone doesn't have the qualifications for the position, it is going to take a great deal of effort on the part of a manager to get them up to speed—hence the "manage tough" line from the earlier quote.

No, you will be better off if you cast a wider net for more applicants.

- Have you **posted the position** everywhere you can?
- Have you told your **professional network** that you have a difficult position to fill and asked for referrals?
- Do you have an **Employee Referral Program** and, if so, are you offering a bonus for a successful hire for this position?

Remember, "It is better to hire smart than manage tough."

Question: You mentioned something called an Employee Referral Program in the last answer. My organization doesn't have such a program. Should we have one, and, if so, how does it work?

Answer: Employee Referral Programs or ERPs can be great sources of applicants, and they have the added bonus of giving you an indication of the morale in your organization.

Start by drafting some program guidelines. The following are typical things contained in such programs that you should consider:

Eligibility. Most programs exempt the HR and recruiting staffs from participating. Some organizations exempt participation for anyone at certain management levels, such as the vice president level or above. It depends on your culture and what you think will work at your organization.

Timing. Some programs are open ended, meaning they are in effect all the time. Others, however, may be time restricted for a certain period or limited to specific, hard-to-fill jobs that are open at a particular time. As with eligibility, this will be dependent on your organization and its needs.

Process. Decide how you want to receive referrals. Ideally, have an easy form that people can fill out online and submit. Decide if you want the referral submission form to require an attached resume.

Rewards. Determine whether you will pay a reward for every resume received or only for qualified applicants, as well as how much you will pay and when. For example, your program will pay $500 (less taxes and eligible deductions) in the paycheck following the applicant being interviewed. If the applicant is hired, you will pay $1,000 in the pay period following the new hire's ninety-day anniversary.

Special circumstances. From time to time, you can put a premium reward on a hard-to-fill position.

There is no one way to put an ERP in place. You can be as creative as you'd like as long as you are consistent in following the rules you set and follow the IRS rules on deductions for applicable taxes.

We mentioned you can get an indication on morale in your organization by having an ERP. On the positive side, employees won't refer someone who isn't qualified as the referral will reflect on them. Conversely, your employees will not refer a friend, relative, or former colleague to your organization if they aren't happy there themselves. If the program isn't meeting your expectations, consider conducting an employee satisfaction survey as discussed in the next section.

Question: What's the difference between an orientation program for new hires and onboarding? Are they interchangeable, or is there something about them that I am missing?

Answer: New-hire orientation programs are a part of an overall **onboarding** strategy, so it is easy to confuse them. Unfortunately, many organizations only do the orientation part of the process and miss the incredible value of a comprehensive onboarding strategy.

Onboarding is a vital component of the employee experience. In fact, the onboarding process starts as soon as the applicant accepts your offer. The onboarding activities are shared between HR and the hiring manager.

The time between when the offer is accepted and when the new hire starts work is a great time to keep in touch with the new hire. HR can send the benefits information and paperwork for completion. The hiring manager can contact the new hire, at least weekly, through calls and a handwritten note of welcome, to keep them excited about starting their new job and to explain what to expect next.

Part of onboarding is having everything ready for the new hire including the technology they'll need. If they will be working remotely on your organization's hardware, be sure it arrives at their home before their first day.

The orientation part of the onboarding process usually takes place on their first day or during their first week and is typically coordinated through or conducted by HR with assistance from other leaders in the organization.

During orientation HR typically completes the I-9 process and goes over the employee handbook and the organization's policies and practices, as well as administrative issues such as payroll. If possible, include department heads of accounting, payroll, IT, security, and others to present their department-specific processes. This is a great way for new hires to meet the leaders of the organization while gaining valuable information.

Don't overlook discussing the company's history, vision, mission, and values. This is a wonderful opportunity to capture the imagination of the new hire—where they see how they fit into the organization and how their skills will be utilized.

An onboarding best practice is to include thirty-sixty-ninety-day evaluations and a data-gathering process where new hires can share their suggestions for improving the onboarding process. This is a valuable source of information for you to tweak your program so that you meet as many needs of new hires as possible.

Question: We have enough to do to find and keep good employees. Now we're being asked to develop job descriptions. It seems like a lot of work, and I don't see what we'd use them for. Why do we need job descriptions?

Answer: Yes, **job descriptions** take some work to develop, but I bet you will be surprised when we share the many ways they will help you hire, onboard, engage, develop, manage performance, and, if needed, terminate a nonperformer. They also play a role in how employees are compensated.

Let's start by talking about hiring. How can you fill a position if you don't know what the job is all about, what the person will do, and what knowledge, skills, and abilities are required? You use job descriptions to craft job postings for your website or to put on social media to find qualified applicants.

When you hire someone from the outside or promote from within, that person will need a job description so they know what they are expected to accomplish. A job description can help a new hire or a newly promoted employee get up to speed quickly, which is a great asset for your organization.

Managers will use the job description when doing a performance review, and if the employee isn't meeting expectations, they have a way to document where they are falling short and develop a path to improving.

I hope we've convinced you that job descriptions add value. Job descriptions are tools that describe the duties and responsibilities of a particular position. They list the purpose of the job and where it fits into the organization. They also list the desired skills needed to be successful in that particular position. They are job specific and not person specific, meaning they describe the job and not the person who does the job. Every job in the organization should have a job description.

Question: You've convinced me that job descriptions are important. What needs to be on a job description?

Answer: While there is no legal requirement of what should be on a job description, there are resources that may help you, such as trade associations or membership groups that have sample job descriptions you can tailor to your particular jobs. However, here are some common and recommended elements to help you get started:

- Summary—a short paragraph that summarizes the purpose of the job and includes the primary responsibilities, the results needed for success, and where the job fits in the organization and/or department.
- Essential functions—those fundamental job-related duties that are necessary to perform this position successfully.
- Nonessential or marginal functions—functions or job-related duties that are incidental or ancillary to the nature of the job.
- Supervisory responsibilities—if applicable.

- Working conditions—the type of atmosphere in which the job is performed, such as unusual or uncomfortable, unpleasant, or dangerous working conditions.
- Minimum qualifications—the education, years of experience, certifications, knowledge, skills, and physical demands of the position, such as lifting requirements, if applicable.
- FLSA status—whether the position is exempt or nonexempt from the overtime provisions of the **Fair Labor Standards Act**.
- Other duties as assigned—a standard practice to ensure and acknowledge that not every task can be listed, and recognizes that duties can shift and change over time.

Be sure to confer with your HR team, who is probably leading the effort to develop job descriptions. They can provide more insight about FLSA status and essential job functions under the **Americans with Disabilities Act** (ADA). While they need your input, they likely will be finalizing the individual job descriptions.

Question: My organization spends a lot of time on a strategic plan, but it doesn't seem to address the people-side of our business. Should we also be doing a workforce plan and if so, what is it and how do we get started?

Answer: It's great your organization has a **strategic plan**, and hopefully it is current, reviewed, and updated as needed. Many organizations take the time and resources to do a strategic plan and then never refer to it again. And, yes, doing a **workforce plan** is highly recommended.

A strategic plan charts the future with broad mission-related targets and milestones. A workforce plan translates that strategic thinking into concrete actions for staffing and employee development needs. When an organization successfully aligns human resources activities with organizational strategies, everyone is on the same page. Keep in mind, your organization needs its people to be proactive. It won't matter how great your product or service is. If you don't have the right people, you won't be successful.

A workforce plan will have impact on just about every HR function in your organization including staffing, compensation, benefits, employee experience, engagement, retention, succession management, employee development, and management/leadership development.

The steps to developing a workforce plan are:

1. Analyze your current workforce in light of any plans for growth or for downsizing.
2. Determine what knowledge, skills, and abilities will be needed to achieve the strategic plans for the next year.
3. Do a gap analysis to see what is missing between your current workforce and your future needs.
4. Plan for how you will fill the gap. Will you train your current workforce, or will you need to go outside to find new talent? Is your organizational structure right for your future plans? If not, what changes do you need to make?
5. How will you implement your workforce plan? What milestones will help move it forward? Obtain the full support of your leadership in order to maximize success of your plan.
6. Communicate the plan to the relevant stakeholders.
7. Develop a strategy to ensure the plan is a living document and reviewed often.

For you, as a manager, a workforce plan gives you a better understanding of the strengths and weaknesses among your staff and provides you with a long-term context.

Question: My organization is experiencing higher than average turnover, and we aren't prepared. What should we be doing to get ahead of retirements and voluntary resignations?

Answer: You've asked a timely question, but in reality, what you've asked about is something organizations should always be doing. It is called **succession management.** It is the way that organizations plan ahead to identify and prepare people who have potential to move into key positions when the incumbent leaves the job.

Having a **succession plan** can help facilitate a smooth continuation of business when positions become vacant. Most succession plans have focused on senior-level positions because of the difficulty of finding replacements with the desired degree of talent needed to fill a key role.

This means you need to know who your organization couldn't live without. Depending on what business or service you are in, key positions may be in sales, marketing, IT, member services, or other key functions specific to your organization.

A succession plan can be done using available technology or simply by using a spreadsheet application, such as Microsoft Excel, allowing any size organization to have a plan in place before one is needed. Here are the steps to follow:

1. Evaluate the skills and potential of your employees.
2. Look at your current organization and your projected growth plans. Also look at potential retirements.
3. Using your analysis of your current staff, see who has the potential to fill an opening due to retirement or growth. You may also have to use your *crystal ball* to project any employee who you think might be considering resigning.
4. Do an Individual Development Plan for anyone you think could fill a key position. If possible, identify more than one person for each key position.
5. Revisit your plan often to be sure it is still viable, and update it as needed.

If you follow these steps, you will be more prepared for the actions of your employees or from unexpected opportunities for growth. However, in our ever-changing world, even a well-crafted succession plan won't always be as helpful as you'd like. People and circumstances will still surprise you. However, you'll be more prepared if you do your succession planning ahead of time.

NAVIGATING THE CHANGING WORKPLACE

Question: I am sure we could improve our communications with applicants if we made better use of mobile technology. Is this something we should look into?

Answer: Definitely. Using **mobile technology** to recruit is having a very large impact on how we hire today. It is an important way to reach people who spend a great deal of time on their phones. People don't just look for job opportunities while they are sitting at their desk on their PC or Mac. They use their phones or tablets from anywhere.

First thing to do is be sure your job postings—on your organization's careers page on your website or posted on LinkedIn or Indeed—are optimized for mobile users. This means you need to take your phone right now and look at how your postings are displayed. If reading them is difficult or if clicking through to your application is impossible to do on a mobile device, you have some work to do with your IT team.

A mobile-friendly experience doesn't simply replicate your desktop site. Incorporate video as much as you can. Record short—under three minutes—comments from your current employees about your culture and what it's like to work for the organization and share them. Invite people to connect with you using your simple application process. Use your social media channels to maximize your visibility.

Don't overlook texting as part of your mobile strategy. Use it to keep applicants informed of your hiring process and their status. Another idea is to text a few questions for the applicant to respond to before an interview. This is a way to engage with the applicant that will show your hiring process is current and strategic.

Mobile recruiting is not just something new to try—it is here to stay.

Question: Now with more people working from home or remotely, we conduct more video interviews. They seem less personal than face-to-face interviews. Any tips for making these interviews more effective?

Answer: Video interviews are especially valuable for screening job candidates. What used to be done by phone is not routinely accomplished on camera, so on camera interviews provide you with more information than you would have collected on the phone.

Just like you would do on the phone or in person, start your video interview with some small talk to help the candidate relax. Stick with a safe subject like the weather to kick things off.

Your comfort factor will help the candidate relax. Smile often and look at the camera so that you're looking into the eyes of the candidate.

As you would in any interview, let the candidate know that you will be taking notes so that if you look away from the camera, they won't think you've lost interest in them.

Be sure your lighting is as good as possible with light in front of you and over your head.

Let the candidate know if, for any reason, you get cut off, you will call them back immediately.

Most people are comfortable on camera now so that this shouldn't be an issue. However, if you are not feeling comfortable, neither will the candidate. This could have a negative impact. So, take time to practice your on-camera skills until you are ready to do an interview that puts the candidate at their best.

Watch body language and eye contact just as you would in an in-person interview. Take time to help the candidate relax, and listen to and observe the candidate. Allow for natural pauses in the conversation. It's the opportunity for you and the candidate to formulate questions and responses. If you concentrate and give the candidate a chance, you will get the information you need.

Question: We now need to conduct onboarding virtually, especially for remote employees, and we don't want to miss an opportunity to

get the new hire started on a positive note. How can we maximize
the experience when we aren't in the same place?

Answer: With technology, **virtual onboarding** can be easy and
make a positive impression on the new hire. For example:

- The hiring manager should contact the new hire immediately
  after the offer is accepted.
- Send the new hire a logo'd item, if available.
- Add the new hire to distribution lists for organizational information before the start date so they feel included.
- Assign a current employee to be a "buddy." Have the buddy
  contact the new hire before the start date. The buddy can
  arrange for other team members to reach out as well.
- Outline what the new hire can expect on day one and through
  the onboarding process—introductory meetings, team meetings, and individual meetings with the manager and others in
  the organization. Include a checklist of all the happenings so
  they can prepare.
- Use an online service like Docusign for everything that needs
  to be signed and returned to HR.
- Notify IT to get necessary equipment ordered, delivered, and
  set up at the employee's home. Leave time for questions and
  answers with IT.
- On the first day, schedule a team lunch and deliver food to
  everyone's homes. Have a virtual introductory session, and
  consider doing a team-building exercise. This gives everyone
  the chance to meet the new hire.
- Train the new hire on any collaboration software as soon as
  possible so they can engage with others immediately.
- Videotape your organization's leadership. Have them introduce
  themselves and share stories about the organization's history
  and culture.

Consider what you would need to know if you were starting at your organization. Talk with a recent hire and ask what worked best for them when they started, and do your best to replicate that experience. Refine the process each time you do, and be as creative as possible.

Question: It became much more difficult to recruit after the tight labor market that followed the 2020 pandemic. I know my organization is taking a proactive approach, but what should I be doing, or doing differently, as a hiring manager to get the best applicants to come to work for us?

Answer: There was a time when managers' primary involvement in hiring was **interviewing** applicants. Then, the focus was on the applicants and why the organization should hire them. You are so right. Much has changed since 2020, and especially when there is a **tight labor market**.

After 2020, applicants became aware that they had choices and more control of the marketplace. That's not necessarily a bad thing when you consider that in the past many organizations treated applicants poorly—not following up after an interview, for example.

Hopefully, your organization's proactive approach includes examining its hiring processes to make them more centered on the applicant. Is it easy for applicants to be found in your applicant tracking system? Are you using your website to tell compelling stories about your culture?

As a manager, you need to sell both the organization and yourself. Applicants today are looking at employers' commitment to and involvement in the community. They are scrutinizing your reputation. You need to sell the positives of these issues during the interview. Give concrete examples that show you incorporate your values into your daily activities and work.

Another important area for applicants is fairness—fair pay and fair work practices. So be prepared to answer questions about these issues.

Sell yourself. What is it like to work for you as a manager? Tell them about a time you demonstrated good management skills. Ask them what they are looking for in a manager. Will you be a good fit for the prospective employee? If it sounds like the tables are turning, they are.

Finally, if the labor market is tight, look beyond the individual's experience and skill. While these are certainly important, you may not find the perfect fit. So, when you evaluate applicants, consider their ambition, potential, and their ability to grow.

Question: My organization used to participate in job fairs, especially industry-specific ones in our community. We were quite successful in attracting applicants and used to hire multiple people at an event. Since job fairs have gone away like so many in-person events, do you have any ideas of other cost-effective things we can do instead?

Answer: You are so right. We are all struggling to find new ways to recruit. One of those new or reinvented recruiting sources is a **virtual job fair.** There are organizations that hold virtual job fairs across the country. Among the more popular are specialized ones that target people with hard-to-find skill sets and others that target minority or female applicants in order to cast a wider net and support diversity efforts.

Virtual job fairs work pretty much like in-person ones but without the long lines for the applicant to only get a few minutes with a recruiter. What's changed? Applicants now schedule time with an employer—usually ten or so minutes—in advance. With up to thirty organizations participating in the virtual job fair, applicants find them to be a great way to maximize their time and appreciate the virtual one-on-one interaction they have with employers. Employers also find them effective.

Like in-person job fairs, the followup after the event is a key to landing the best talent available. Employers need a good tracking system so that they can quickly respond to anyone interviewed. Those who are not selected to move onto the next level should be notified as soon as possible after the event, and those who require further attention should be contacted immediately to schedule the next interview.

Give virtual job fairs a try and see if they work for you.

Question: There is an emphasis on diversity these days and the need to have diverse candidates and a diverse workforce. Isn't this just affirmative action, and aren't organizations sacrificing qualified candidates if the focus is just on diversity?

Answer: You've got two questions here, so let's start with the first one and explain affirmative action. Organizations that contract to do business with the federal government (and in some cases state and local governments) are required to have **affirmative action programs**. This means they have to take specific steps to employ and advance in employment individuals in certain protected classes—women and people of color or minorities.

Affirmative action is providing **equal employment opportunities** to everyone, giving full consideration to women and minorities in all areas of employment, understanding where protected classes are not fully represented in your workforce, and taking proactive steps to attract and retain individuals in protected classes.

Moving on to your second question, affirmative action does not mean providing **preferences**, using **quotas,** or lowering job qualifications. In the hiring process, this is where affirmative action, which is mandatory for government contractors, intersects with organizations' diversity efforts, which are voluntary.

Taking proactive steps to attract a diverse pool of candidates means *casting a wider net* in your recruitment practices. If you're looking to hire engineers, for example, there are organizations, websites, and job boards that represent minority engineers, such as the National Society of Black Engineers. There are excellent sources of qualified minority candidates in a variety of professions. With tools like Google and the internet, these sources are easy to identify, and there are many of them available.

If you're defining diversity in terms of preferences or quotas—we've got to hire two minorities this quarter—you're definitely on the wrong track. And if you're using someone's race, for example, to make a hiring decision, you'll likely not make the best hire. Preferential hiring can lead to discrimination, and yes, it's possible to discriminate against white men. Preferences and quotas were never the intention of affirmative action and should not be the approach taken in diversity hiring. The most important thing is to hire the best-qualified candidates available. Just be sure you're looking for them in all the right and diverse places.

Question: I feel as if I finally understand the Millennials we have working for us and now, along comes Generation Z. What do we need to know to successfully recruit them?

Answer: Yes, this is a whole new group of people who we know need to understand so we can be at the top of the line to recruit them. Here are some tips:

- Your culture and your employment brand are everything to **Generation Z**. As digital natives, they will have done extensive research on your organization before they even *consider* applying for a job. They'll be looking at many social platforms. Therefore, it is important that anything written or said about your organization aligns with what you say on your website. For example, stress your commitment to your employees and their development, but only if it is true. You don't want applicants getting one story from your social media and finding out things are different on the inside of the organization. Your brand and your culture must align.
- Generation Z, like pretty much all your staff members, is seeking flexibility. So if you want to attract them, this should be front and center in your job posts.
- This generation is focused on their career and personal development. They are looking for jobs where the culture

supports mentoring, coaching, on the job training—more commonly now called microlearning opportunities—and constant feedback. With this interest on how your job opportunity will expand their career, it is important that your job posts and your website's career page showcase development opportunities.

- Generation Z employees want to work for socially conscious organizations. So if your organization supports specific causes, be sure to include stories and pictures of what you do. This generation wants an organization's culture to align with their interests and their values.

- Connecting to the people in your organization is especially important to Generation Z staff members. They are looking for a culture of inclusion, so it's equally important your diversity, equity, and inclusion (DEI) efforts are described and observable.

As we have learned over time, with each generation there comes challenges. Hope this helps you get started with the latest one—Generation Z.

Question: There seems to be a great deal of recent discussion regarding college degrees and whether they are necessary. We've required them for so many of our positions, especially technical positions, but are they really needed to do the job?

Answer: You may be onto something: Do organizations require a **college degree** because it is necessary to do the job, or due to tradition and aversion to change? I can't answer for your organization, but here is something to think about as you decide what's right for you.

Requiring a degree because *we've always done it* is probably keeping competent people from applying to your organization. In times of labor scarcity, this practice can cost organizations significant money by keeping positions open longer than if you didn't have the degree requirement.

Only approximately 35 percent of Americans have a four-year degree. Because organizations have, perhaps, required degrees when they might not have been necessary, organizations may have paid a lot of salary that might not have been necessary if the position had been open to a non-degreed individual.

This is a great opportunity to look at each of your positions, especially the entry-level ones. Carefully evaluate the educational experience currently required and whether it still makes sense today. If yes, you're good to go. However, if someone without a degree, or perhaps someone with an associate degree, could do the job, make the change.

Also keep in mind, especially for more experienced-level positions, that you could be screening out qualified candidates with excellent experience who are quite capable of doing the job. This has long been the EEOC's position on degree requirements, their concern stemming from the potential of creating adverse impact (or unintentional discrimination) against protected classes. This is why position descriptions often state a degree requirement or equivalent experience.

Of course, there are positions for which degrees and certifications are necessary, especially in certain industries. You most likely want your CFO to be a Certified Public Accountant (CPA), but not everyone in your accounting department needs to have that level of education.

Focus on what your candidate knows versus where they learned what they know. Remember that people can learn valuable skills in many different places, including on the job. Make any necessary changes in what you require for positions where a degree isn't required and test it out. You can always reinstate the degree requirement should you need to. Good luck.

AVOIDING LEGAL PITFALLS

Question: A colleague recently shared a suggestion received from a financial advisor. Never hire employees for your company. Rather

always engage people as 1099 contractors, and you can save on taxes. Is this a valid suggestion?

Answer: Well, an organization can certainly save on payroll taxes with this approach, **except** it will likely incur liability for misclassifying employees as independent contractors. If you misclassify a worker as an **independent contractor** you can be required to pay back taxes and possibly benefits.

In making the determination, the IRS will look at the degree of control an organization has over the individual. That degree of control falls into three categories:

- Behavioral control, which includes factors such as the type and degree of instruction provided, whether the individual is subject to any evaluation, and whether any training is provided.
- Financial control, which includes factors such as whether the individual makes their services available to others, the individual's opportunity for profit or loss, the degree of investment the individual makes (such as purchases their own computer), the extent of unreimbursed expenses the individual incurs (independent contractors are generally liable for their own expenses), and how the individual is paid (salary versus a fee for services which are generally invoiced).
- Type of relationship that considers whether the organization provides the individual typical employee benefits, the existence of a contract defining the terms and conditions of the relationship, the expectation of the continuance of the relationship (indefinite or for a specific, finite period—for example, to perform certain projects), and whether or not the services the individual provides are key aspects of regular business activity (such as ongoing activities) over which the organization would likely have greater control.

Check the IRS's website and do a search for independent contractors. They provide information and publications on how to determine if a worker is an employee or independent contractor. Be sure you also check with your legal advisor.

Question: During the course of an interview, a candidate voluntarily disclosed that they had suffered a nervous breakdown. They had some of the technical skills we were looking for, but their communication skills, which are critical for the position, are weak. Two others who interviewed them, but are unaware of the medical issue, agree they are not a top contender for the job. Knowing about their past medical condition, should I be concerned about not hiring them since they are probably covered by the ADA?

Answer: You have good insights and are right to take all this information into consideration. Let's begin by looking at the requirements of the **Americans with Disabilities Act (ADA)**.

Under the ADA, you cannot discriminate on the basis of a physical or mental disability. When it comes to hiring, that means you can't base your decision on that protection. Having information that isn't relevant to the job—especially information you didn't request—can be cause for concern. In evaluating this candidate, if you were thinking, "They could have another breakdown, and it would impact the department, so let's not hire them," you would be opening the door to **discrimination**.

However, from what you described, there seems to be consensus among all the interviewers that this candidate lacks a critical skill, perhaps even an **essential function**, for the job. (An essential function is a primary job duty required in a job that a qualified individual must be able to perform with or without an accommodation.)

In making any hiring decision, each candidate should be evaluated against the requirements of the job, including any essential functions. If your organization has well-defined job or position descriptions that document these requirements, and if every candidate is evaluated against them by all interviewers, and if these evaluations are well documented, it is likely that your organization would be successful if faced with a discrimination claim in this circumstance.

It's always a good idea to consult with your HR and legal advisors about the type of concerns you expressed. They will be more familiar with your organization's policies and practices. Concerns such as yours present a good opportunity for conducting reviews of your employment practices.

Question: We're recruiting for an executive position in our nonprofit, and I'm on the selection committee. One of my staff members happened to see the name of a candidate and sounded an alarm. It seems this candidate worked for a friend's employer, and there were rumors he'd engaged in behavior that was considered sexual harassment. Should I bring this information to our CEO or just ignore it?

Answer: Congratulations for being included as part of the selection for someone to fill an executive position. It's evident that you take this responsibility seriously.

You don't say how the candidates being considered were presented to the selection committee, but a reasonable assumption is that a **search firm** may have been retained. If that's the case, hopefully, they did some advance vetting. Has this candidate, or any of them, been interviewed yet? Where you are in the process may determine next steps, especially for the candidate in question.

Issues involving workplace gossip always have to be considered very carefully, and the information you have right now is based on rumors. However, that doesn't necessarily mean it should be discounted. Consider the following: You say nothing, the individual is hired, the rumors turn out to be true, and they begin sexually harassing staff members not long after they start working for your organization.

If that scenario played out, the organization could be facing not only claims of **sexual harassment**, but also negligent hiring. **Negligent hiring** is a common-law (or judge-made) claim that alleges the employer knew or should have known an employee posed a risk. One reason references are checked, candidates are carefully screened, and background checks are conducted is to assess risks. This is especially important when executives are being hired—they will be in positions where job duties can be exploited.

It would be wise to bring the information you have to your CEO, stressing that it is based on rumor. If this candidate advances in the process and becomes a serious contender, the CEO, any search firm, and HR will be best positioned to conduct all the necessary checks and screens, with guidance, if necessary, from legal advisors.

Question: I've heard about administering tests to applicants to avoid costly hiring mistakes. This seems pretty straightforward, but I'm getting resistance from my HR team, which is reluctant to do so. Is there something I'm missing?

Answer: **Employment testing,** whether for applicants or current employees seeking promotions, is more complex than it seems. Organizations must evaluate all their selection processes to ensure they are free of discrimination.

Disparate treatment, or intentional discrimination—for example, only hiring white males—would not be a factor in employment tests. However, **disparate impact** (or adverse impact) must be considered. This form of discrimination occurs when the results of a practice, or a test, has a negative, more inhibiting effect on members of certain groups—**protected classes**, such as people of color or women. While a test or practice may seem neutral on its face, it's effect might be to screen out people in protected classes at a greater rate than others.

To ensure against any discriminatory effects, tests must establish **reliability,** which is the ability of an instrument to measure results consistently. So, if an applicant takes a test more than once, the scores should be similar each time for the test to be reliable.

Tests must also establish **validity**, which is the ability to measure what is intended to be measured. Validating a test considers what the test measures and how well the test measures it. Does it identify those individuals more likely to be successful and eliminate those individuals less likely to be successful on a particular job?

Studies to determine reliability and validity are usually conducted by specialized consulting firms or industrial psychologists. They examine the job elements actually performed and prerequisites for the job and compare them to the information sought on the test to ensure a direct correlation exists. The process to do this is lengthy and can be expensive.

While there are many assessment tools and employment tests available, they need to be selected carefully and monitored frequently to ensure they are still valid and reliable, and to ensure you don't run the risk of litigation if a selection decision is challenged.

CLOSING THOUGHTS

It doesn't matter how great your product or service is if you don't have the staff to make it happen. Casting a wide net for qualified applicants and then treating them with respect and dignity in the interview process will position your firm to be the best you can be. The next step is to bring them into your culture with great care in your onboarding process. Read the next section of this book for insights to help you engage and retain your talent.

CREATING A POSITIVE EMPLOYEE EXPERIENCE

YOU HAVE DONE your absolute best to attract and hire a fantastic group of new hires to your organization and have provided them with a great experience in the hiring process. Your next job is to create the best possible experience for them in their new role as employees (or whatever you call your people). Their time with your organization is like a journey with lots of moving parts. What makes a positive employee experience? A strong culture where leaders live the organization's values and listen to the needs of their people.

This section answers a lot of questions about how you can make the employee experience positive so that the employees do great work, make valuable contributions to your success, and want to keep working for you for a long time. We discuss onboarding both in person and virtual and introduce the significance of meeting people's emotional compensation needs along with other ways to ensure employee engagement.

Question: I keep hearing about the employee experience, but am not sure I know what it is. Can you please share some details of what it means and why it's important?

Answer: The **employee experience** is simply the sum of all interactions your employees have with your organization. It is the structure and, more importantly, your culture and how your employees perceive your overall organization and their role in it. Sometimes it's described as the "journey an employee takes with your organization."

How many times have you heard a leader say that their employees are their greatest asset? The employee experience is putting some action behind those words. The best way to find out what would make a good employee experience is to ask your staff what is important to them. You need to listen carefully to their answers and take action whenever possible.

By focusing on experiences over processes, savvy employers create moments that are intuitive and adaptable to what really matters to your employees and to your business goals.

The employee experience starts in the hiring process. Consider:

- What do you share on your website about your culture?
- How do you treat applicants in the hiring process?
- What is your onboarding process like?
- What do your employees know about your mission and your values?
- Does your leadership live your values?
- How flexible is your workplace?
- How are employees recognized and rewarded for living your values?

These are some of the many questions you want to explore as you consider how good your organization's employee experience strategy is. When you know what is important to your staff, then involve your management team and your leadership in focusing on creating the absolute best journey you can create.

Don't overlook the importance of developing the skills of your employees. Be sure your communication strategy includes one-on-one conversations with every employee to measure their well-being. Being asked the question, "how are you?" and having the answer heard will go a long way toward improving the experience of your valued people. Try it and not just once—make it a part of your management routine, and watch how it improves your team's morale.

Question: I want to get my employees off to a good start. Are there things we should be doing in the first few days and weeks to ensure their employee experience is as good as it can be?

Answer: Absolutely. Those first few days of **onboarding** are critical to your new hire getting off to a good start. Yes, some things will be the same for everyone, but many of the preparations you make will be specific to a particular individual, so start with a plan for each person.

On their first day, whether it is in-person or virtual, at a minimum, here are some things to have in place for the new employee:

- Work area should be set up with the appropriate equipment. If the employee will be working virtually, have any technology they need delivered to their home in advance.
- Written materials and instructions, such as setting passwords, voice mail instructions, and strategic plan, should be ready and waiting or provided ahead of time.
- Whom-to-call information should be available.

Actions to consider during their first day include:

- Assign a *buddy* who can be part of the welcoming process and also a valuable resource to answer questions for them as well.

- Be available for as much of a new hire's first day as possible in order to answer questions and provide information on what they can expect during their first few days and weeks.
- Take them to lunch on the first day, or if they are working virtually, have lunch delivered to their home and arrange to eat with them remotely.

During their first week, introduce them to more people each day and give them more background information. Spreading it out over the week gives them a chance to absorb it.

Check in on the last day of the week to get feedback on how their week has gone and suggestions for what might have been more helpful. Advise them if you plan periodic check-ins at thirty, sixty, and ninety days, which is a recommended way to keep in close contact.

Don't forget to let them know how happy you are that they have joined your organization and that you look forward to working with them and to the contributions they will make.

The best way to ensure your new hire gets off to a great start is to think back to your first days of employment with the organization and what you wish you'd known, and then do it for your new hires.

Question: I'm looking for some new ideas to keep my employees engaged and motivated. I don't have much of a budget to offer monetary rewards or gifts. Do you have any suggestions of simple things I can do?

Answer: Here are a couple of suggestions for you to try to increase **employee engagement:**

- Solving all the issues facing your team at any one time can be exhausting for any manager. Ask your employees for suggestions to improve productivity or resolve a particularly tricky issue with a customer or client. Take time at each staff meeting or in one-on-one meetings with your employees to ask for their ideas. Simply put—give them a voice.

- Consider asking your employees what processes, reports, or paperwork get in their way. You may learn that some of what you think is motivating them isn't and is counterproductive. You certainly don't want to be a demotivating manager.
- Refrain from immediately rejecting ideas. Nothing will shut down new ideas quicker than being told "that won't work" or "we've tried that before." Instead, take the time to consider or even brainstorm these ideas. You might be surprised at the results.

It may take a while for them to be comfortable making suggestions, but give it time. You may solve a problem while finding a new way to energize your staff. And be sure to read the next question about **emotional compensation.**

Question: Keeping employees engaged and motivated is always a challenge. Are there any new approaches that I can consider?

Answer: Engagement and motivation are integral for employee retention. Higher wages, hiring bonuses, and increased benefits packages all sound like possible solutions. However, there are plenty of examples of employees leaving good-paying jobs because of dissatisfaction.

Here's another thing to consider—what's your work environment, or your corporate culture, like? Is it having the impact you want on your employees? If not, consider another form of compensation—**emotional compensation.**

Emotional compensation is based on seven universal human needs—needs that allow people to thrive at work. The following is a list of needs and some examples of what a manager can do.

- Respect—asking employees their opinions and seriously listening to their responses.
- Recognition—thanking employees for their work and letting them know that their contributions bring value.

- Belonging—engaging in team building and encouraging employees' creative ideas. Creating opportunities for your employees to feel connected—to their managers, to their coworkers, and to the work they perform.
- Autonomy—giving employees flexibility to do their jobs, which includes flexibility of where they work and when they work, and allowing a degree of control over working conditions and processes.
- Personal growth—sharing your knowledge and experience and suggesting resources such as YouTube videos, Ted Talks, blogs, webinars, and articles.
- Meaning—making people feel proud of their work and your organization through alignment with your purpose, vision, and values. Assigning them projects that have an impact and make a difference.
- Progress—providing frequent feedback, following up on their learning activities, and assigning new projects and tasks (stretch assignments) that could lead to new opportunities.

When these needs are met—at least some of them—people perceive they are being seen and supported and connections develop. When connections develop and are maintained, your chances of keeping valued team members increases dramatically.

Question: I think I am beginning to understand the value of having employees who are engaged in their work and in our organization. However, I don't know how to measure the degree to which my employees are engaged or when enough of them are engaged. Is there a goal I should be aiming for?

Answer: Well, the short answer is 100 percent, but that is most likely a hard target to hit in our very competitive world. Seriously, why would you not want to have all your employees fully engaged in their work and your organization?

An **engaged employee** is defined as one who is fully absorbed by and enthusiastic about the work and who takes positive action to further the organization's reputation and interests. An engaged employee has a positive attitude toward the organization and its values. Contrast that employee with one who is not engaged, or worse, actively disengaged. I think you will agree that the more engaged staff members you have, the more success your organization will have.

Aim for 100 percent and keep trying to close the gap between engaged and **disengaged employees.**, Use all your skills and available organizational tools to energize and engage your team to maximize their productivity. Measure engagement by doing surveys from time to time, but between surveys, use your listening skills to help you understand the level of engagement your people have.

Don't forget that engagement levels can fluctuate. For example, you may find people are highly engaged at the beginning of a new and exciting project, but if there isn't meaningful progress, such as significant milestones not being met, they may lose some of their initial involvement and enthusiasm. That's a good time for you to stop and evaluate what went wrong, and what corrections need to take place so that the project is on a successful path and engagement increases. This will help you retain staff.

Employee engagement is so important to **retention** and a positive **employee experience**. There are many examples throughout the book, especially in this section. We encourage you to keep reading.

Question: Like most organizations, mine has a mission statement and values, but organizational values can get lost in the day-to-day work we do. What can we do to make sure our values help us stay grounded and as productive as possible?

Answer: You are so right. Values may be easy words to speak or share in communication, but they have to be living and fluid. Here are some ideas of things you can do as a manager and as an organization to ensure your **mission statement** and **organizational values** have meaning.

- Remind employees often of your values—what they are and what they mean. A great way to do this is by sharing stories of employees demonstrating your values in action. One organization rewards employees when they are observed living a value.
- Add your values to your email signature line for internal and external communication. Be sure they are front and center on your social media posts and on your website.
- Select a value to focus on for a month. Share examples of why it is one of your values in your department staff meetings.
- Demonstrate your values every day through your behavior. If managers and the leadership aren't living those values every day, your employees certainly won't live them either, and you risk derailing your organization in a very quick time frame.

Values should be fluid. They are not something you put in place on day one and never touch again. You certainly don't want them to be empty jargon that doesn't reflect where your organization is today. If your organization is not already doing so, suggest to the leadership that your values be reevaluated from time to time. Solicit input from your staff, and keep them in the forefront of internal and external communications.

Question: Hybrid workplaces and hybrid workforces didn't exist when I was in business school, and they certainly didn't teach us about them. How do managers make sense of all these new ways of working?

Answer: Hybrid **workforces** and **remote working** seemed like the *Wild West* to many business leaders when they were forced to adapt them during the 2020 pandemic. Savvy leaders and successful organizations discovered how to not only make them work, but how employees could thrive in these new arrangements.

One secret to success is understanding and accommodating the needs of individual employees—those who live near the physical office and those in more remote settings, or those who are working from home with small children. Ultimately, it's a people management issue—and people management is shared across the organization, especially larger ones.

Let's start by looking at what organizations have done to adjust to **hybrid work arrangements**, then look at the role of the individual manager.

Constant or periodic **employee surveys** can be conducted to elicit their feedback, which helps you understand how they are adapting and whether their Individual needs are being met. **Mobile technology** can help with administering quick and frequent surveys.

Another important factor is making constant adjustments to hybrid plans. One reason why: Employees' circumstances change, and these changes likely affect their preferences about where they want to work. Another reason plans can pivot and change: Organizations have to consider how best to integrate and mentor new hires.

What can a manager do to support its organization's efforts?

- Talk to your staff and listen to their needs. You're on the front line of people management, and you can augment survey data with facts and stories.
- Find out what challenges your staff is facing. If you can't address them directly, bring them to the leadership. Either way, follow up with your employees with possible solutions.
- Don't get discouraged if their needs change. Be flexible and adapt to meet the changes. The ability to adapt to change is an important management competency.

The next question is about retaining talent, so keep reading, and look for the questions throughout the book regarding "Navigating the Changing Workplace."

Question: After working very hard to find and hire the best talent available, it is discouraging when people resign. What can we do to hang on to as many of our employees for as long as possible?

Answer: You are so right. Not only does turnover cost your organization money and time, it also has an impact on morale as much of our work is done in teams. When someone leaves, it takes time to replace them, and their work falls to others. As you point out, it is a better option to **retain your staff** than to replace them.

If you're not already doing **exit interviews**, this is a good time to start. Don't have a direct supervisor do the exit interview. HR or an outside consultant should conduct the interview and ask a series of **open-ended questions** designed to get to the issues that caused the employee to resign.

Look for trends in what you hear in exit interviews. For example, if you hear that your benefits package is lacking a critical component, do some research to see what your competition offers their employees.

Take action to mitigate the negatives you hear from exiting employees and monitor the impact those changes have on your turnover.

There is another way to gather information to prevent turnover. It is called a **stay interview.** It is simple—ask people why they stay with your organization. Try to get as much information as possible by asking follow-up questions. For example, if the employee says they stay working for you because the benefits package is so good, ask for more specifics so that you will be able to use that information when interviewing new employees. If you hear from several people that they stay with you because their manager is a good listener and allows for creativity in their department, you can let that manager know their work is appreciated. Also, share that information with the rest of your management team to encourage them to be good listeners and to encourage creativity.

Using stay interviews to develop **retention strategies** will help your organization to keep your employees happy to stay working with you. Give it a try.

Question: As a new manager, building trust with your team is so important, and I think I've done a good job at doing so initially. However, maintaining that trust is something I want to continue doing. Can you give me any tips for doing so?

Answer: Maintaining **trust** among your staff is one of the most important things a manager must do to ensure everyone's success. To gauge how you're doing, one thing to consider: How many times do you *tell* someone to do something as opposed to how many times do you *ask* them to do something? There's a big difference.

When you tell a staff member to do something, you're giving them a directive or instructions about how to carry out a task. At least that's how the staff member is likely to perceive it. At a minimum, the work will get done, likely the way you want it accomplished. This approach sends the message, "It's my way or the highway," which stifles ideas and creativity.

When you ask someone to do something, whether it's to carry out a task or to solve a problem, you're giving them the flexibility to accomplish something using their own resources and initiative. The message it sends: "I trust your instincts and abilities to accomplish the task or solve the problem without direction from me." As a bonus, their solution may be a better one than yours. It may sound like a cliche, but when you ask someone to do something, you're empowering them to bring their creativity to the workplace.

There's a bonus to this approach, especially if you are concerned that they might not get it right. It presents an excellent opportunity for **coaching**. Beyond building confidence and trust, it:

- Creates more opportunities to develop people, hear their ideas, and show them that they matter and contribute to the organization.
- Increases employee, and in some cases client, retention.
- Tells employees they add value to the organization.
- Is a long-term investment.

If the employee's approach or solution isn't necessarily the best fit, be patient and have confidence in your own coaching ability.

Question: I understand what was said in the last question about the difference between telling and asking and how that builds trust. However, there are times when you have to provide instructions or deliver a directive, especially when you're explaining things to a new employee, or to a group of employees in a new situation. How do you do that without sounding like you're giving them orders?

Answer: You make a good point. While no manager ever wants to come across as if they are giving commands, there are times you may have to be in command of a situation. That's where emotional intelligence comes into play and why it's so important to be aware of how you deliver messages to your team, especially if you're **delegating** new work.

Have a clear understanding of what you need to explain. For example:

- If you're explaining a routine task to a new employee, and things have to be done a certain way, explain why. Let them know you are not trying to take away any autonomy on their part, but that there might be adverse effects if standard procedures are not followed.
- If you're explaining new processes or requirements to existing employees, explain the rationale behind it. If there are new technologies or requirements that are driving the changes, explain what they are and how—especially in the case of technology—they are likely to make things more efficient.

Depending on the nature of the task and considering what you need to explain, describing or taking the opportunity to demonstrate what needs to be done gives the employees the opportunity to visualize themselves doing the task successfully. It also provides them the opportunity to observe and ask questions. You don't want to leave the employees on their own to figure it out if it's something that has no room for creativity nor error.

Finally, and most importantly, explain how their work (or this task) fits in with other work. It will let them know they are making a contribution to the overall organization and give them a sense of purpose.

Question: We used to periodically conduct employee surveys. Should we continue that practice and if so, how can we get employees to participate, and how should we share the results with our staff?

Answer: Asking for your employee's opinions is always a good idea, especially in changing times. Don't do an **employee survey** unless you are prepared to act on the information shared by your staff. This does not mean you have to take action on every suggestion made, but you should be prepared to review and consider the information you collect and report back to your staff.

If you can't take action on a suggestion, let your staff know you heard them and explain the business reason why it can't be implemented at this time. If you ignore a suggestion or idea from an employee or group of employees, odds are you will never again have a successful survey and the level of trust will be eroded.

Communication is the key to getting a good response to the survey, but so is trust. If your employees don't hold your leadership in high esteem and/or trust them, odds are they will ignore your questions.

Use every means possible to publicize the survey. Involve managers and supervisors and ask them to encourage their staff to participate.

Here is some suggested wording to announce your survey. Obviously, you'll use wording appropriate to your organization:

"To honor our commitment to our valued employees, we're asking for your opinions and candid feedback. We will be using your feedback both to learn, but also to develop action plans for improvement of our working environment. Your individual responses will be completely confidential, and the results will be analyzed by an outside consulting firm so that all information will remain private."

When you get the results, deal with them in a way that is transparent. This doesn't mean you share every word, but put together some themes, and, as quickly as possible, share the major themes with your staff. Then, assemble teams to put action plans together for each theme. Consider using staff to work on the action plans as a team building activity and to let your employees know you trust them and value their expertise.

Once you successfully complete a survey and your employees see you listen to them, odds are they will actively participate in future surveys. Good luck.

Question: What are some possible questions we can ask on an employee survey?

Answer: One way of gathering information from an **employee survey** is to present specific statements and ask them to rate each using a rating scale of 1 to 10 with 1 meaning they totally disagree with the statement and ten means they totally agree. Employees can use any number from 1 to 10. You also may want to add a place for respondents to give you examples of why they used a particular rating.

You can use any of the software products available, such as SurveyMonkey, or design your own survey. Make the survey easy to use, and limit your questions to a number you think will work for your employee population.

Carefully craft the questions to be asked and do your best to ask many of the same questions each time you do a survey. This will allow you to measure progress made or alert you to concerns that intensify from year to year.

Here are some possible questions:

- Our leadership has a clear vision for our future.
- My manager keeps me informed of changes in the organization.
- My manager is open to new ideas.
- I have confidence in the leadership of this organization.

- I am proud to work here.
- My compensation package (salary and benefits) is competitive with jobs in my field.
- I enjoy working here.
- I have the tools I need to do my job.
- I am given feedback as often as I need it.
- I know what's expected of me at work.
- The organization allows me to have a good work/life balance.
- I can make a contribution here.
- I receive recognition for my work when appropriate.
- I hope to work here for a long time.
- I can develop my skills here.

Surveys can be a valuable source of information for you if you ask good questions and take action if and when you can. Don't forget to share good business reasons if you can't act on a suggestion.

Question: My organization is serious about encouraging our workforce to be more engaged in the work we do and in our mission. Engagement is a critical component of our retention strategy since it has a major impact on our productivity. What are some strategies for us to increase our employee engagement levels?

Answer: Yes, you are right about the importance of **employee engagement** to your employee **retention strategy.** Unfortunately, there is not one way to engage your staff, but there are some suggestions for you and your leadership to try.

Communication. How frequently are front line managers having one-on-one conversations with their employees and checking in on projects or work assignments status? Are managers holding staff meetings to keep the team up to date on news from your leadership team. Does your leadership meet with the entire organization as often as needed to let everyone know how the organization is doing and what might be coming down the road?

Transparency. Employees want to know if there is bad news. Transparency is extremely important to employee engagement. Be as honest with your team as the situation allows.

Recognition. Let people know often where they fit in the organization and why their job matters in the overall performance of the organization. Find ways to recognize employees for their contributions. There are many no and low-cost ways to reward people for performance-related action, but don't forget the most important words you can speak to an employee are *thank you*. A sincere and timely thanks goes a long way toward building up engagement.

Trust. When you make a commitment, do your absolute best to keep it. If you can't, share the reasons why and apologize. Let your employees see your vulnerable side when appropriate. Share your shortcomings so you are seen as a human being. Trust is a critical element of an engaged workforce, so always keep your word.

Rewards. Be sure your total rewards programs are as good as you can make them. Pay fairly, and be sure your benefits plans are designed with your workforce in mind.

Employee engagement starts in the hiring and onboarding processes and continues throughout the employment relationship. Never miss an opportunity to share and reinforce your values to applicants and employees alike. Get them excited about where they can make a contribution to your organization, and watch your engagement soar.

Question: I have a couple of superstars whom I would be lost without. Is there anything I can do to hang on to them as long as possible?

Answer: Yes, you can **re-recruit superstars** to your organization. If these people are so important to your work and/or your organization, you probably know a lot about them, far more than you knew when you first recruited them. Use that additional knowledge and apply the same techniques you did to hire them.

Take some time with them to do a **stay interview,** discussed in an earlier question in this section. Get their perspective on what they like and don't like about their work and your organization. What are they passionate about both at work and personally? What are their career objectives now that they've been in the job for a while?

Put together a strategy for each of your superstars, trying to meet as many of their needs or desires as possible. For example, if they desire to stay with your organization but transfer to other departments, consider working with your colleagues in other departments to see if there is a possible transfer opportunity or a task force they might join. Be as creative and personal as possible. Personal attention is highly impactful.

If you find that your superstars are looking for more interaction with your senior leadership, consider setting up a series of meetings, video conferences or lunches with senior staff. Do this in a casual setting if possible, and encourage the superstars to know it is safe for them to ask questions. This kind of session will also give your leadership an opportunity to get to know your employees which will be an asset for you in your succession planning efforts.

These are excellent ways to connect with your best employees on a human level. You may find out that an employee has a personal goal to finish a degree or get an advanced degree. If your organization has a tuition reimbursement plan, you can encourage the employee to apply for the benefit and even help them find a program that will meet their needs.

One of the most difficult roles managers play is retaining staff, but no one manager does that alone. Be as creative as possible to find strategies to retain your talented employees, and work with your fellow managers to utilize every idea available to be successful.

NAVIGATING THE CHANGING WORKPLACE

Question: As we are learning about the new realities of the changing workplace, one thing I keep hearing is that work has to become asynchronous. What does asynchronous work mean and what does it look like?

Response: Let's start with the type of work we were used to before things changed quickly and drastically. People went to work in offices, spent face time with colleagues, and used the tools, equipment, and space their employer provided. Everyone worked the same schedule. Even then, teams could be located in different time zones or regions of the world, and yet, they were expected to work in a manner with everything happening at the same time.

Is this **synchronous work** model working effectively in today's environment? No, and it probably didn't in the past when workers in different time zones or on different continents were faced with constant distractions—messaging from apps or pings throughout all hours of the night—and anxiety due to expectations for immediate responses.

How can things improve? Consider an **asynchronous work** model with people working on their own time and where they are allowed to complete their work and answer colleagues when it's convenient, of course within a reasonable time frame. Everything is not happening at the same time. Team members can set tasks and deadlines, or hand off tasks, for their peers without the expectation of response right away. The only expectation is that the work be completed in a timely manner.

How do you transition to this new model? There are tools to allow asynchronous work to occur, such as taskmaster apps rather than simple messaging apps. Research some of these tools. Reduce or remove meetings—especially video ones—and save meeting time for more complicated topics, discussions, and brainstorming.

Flexibility is the future, and organizations need to accept and adapt to distributed work models if they want to retain their talent. Employees want more flexibility, and this includes not only where they work, but when and how the work gets done. Balancing synchronous and asynchronous communication supports flexibility.

Is the way your organization working still working? It may be time to reevaluate to determine what model results in the most productive and least-stressed employees.

Question: Technology has certainly risen in importance since 2020. Now the use of mobile technology is being encouraged. How can our organization best use it, especially in our people-management efforts?

Response: Mobile technology and mobile apps have so many uses today, and as the technology evolves, they are becoming easier and more efficient to use.

Consider mobile web apps that don't require the user to download another app to their phone. They live in the cloud and are accessible via text message, link, or QR code. They don't require IT assistance and are easy to use and manage from your phone.

How does mobile technology help with people management? **Text messaging** is a fast and effective way to communicate with your team. Text alerts can be sent for open enrollment, employee recognition, meeting reminders, and links to surveys.

Beyond simple communication, the use of mobile apps keeps employees connected and engaged. Organizations are using them to support **employee development** through gamification and microlearning which we discuss in Section 4. There are also apps that support managers with performance management tasks and duties.

Benefits are important to employees. Mobile technology can be used to share information through videos and even attention-grabbing memes and GIFS.

Let's not overlook how mobile technology supports **recruiting and onboarding** of new employees. Maintaining communication with candidates is crucial, and text messaging is an excellent way to keep in touch during the interview process with interview reminders and updates, for example. The technology can also link job seekers to relevant lists of job openings. Mobile apps can streamline many aspects of the onboarding process too, linking new hires to benefit information, contact directories, and the organization's intranet, saving time and administrative effort.

Don't be surprised to learn that mobile technology can also help organizations maintain their positive cultures. Consider keeping employees engaged with inspiring video content, supportive training resources, messages from leadership, and even selfie portals for employees to upload photos, all on a mobile-friendly platform.

If you have an internal HR team, work closely with them to leverage this ever-changing and emerging technology. It will free up your time and provide the opportunity to become more engaged with your team on a one-on-one basis.

Question: With more and more employees working remotely either full time or part time, I'm struggling with keeping track of everyone's work and whereabouts. For example, I've got one team member who often does not answer the phone when I call, although eventually they do return my call. I don't want to micromanage my staff. Can you provide any tips?

Answer: Some managers struggled making the switch to remote working. They were used to seeing everyone in one place. However, **hybrid working arrangements** are not going away. To be successful managers have to be **flexible and agile**.

In order to adjust, start by examining your **expectations** of this particular employee and all your staff members for that matter. Then ask yourself if your expectations are reasonable. For example:

- Do you expect employees to drop everything and answer your call at the moment you call?
- Are you annoyed if they've taken time to tend to a personal matter?
- Is it critical that they accomplish work-related tasks during standard working hours?

Remember back to when everyone was in the office. Employees might have stepped away from their desks to attend meetings or confer with colleagues, or left for personal reasons.

The important issues you should examine and address next are:

- Have you communicated expectations—e.g., return calls or emails within a certain time period?

- Are there certain blocks of time during the day that employees are expected to be available?
- If a team member needs to be away—medical appointments, for instance—do they know they need to advise you?
- Do you specify timelines for tasks and projects? Are there checkpoints along the way?
- Are employees completing projects and tasks in a quality and timely manner?

Don't lose sight of your management responsibility to ensure that the work gets accomplished. The new work arrangements that have emerged have shown that employees are happier and more productive. The bonus for you is that you don't have to spend your time with needless tracking. You can expand your management horizons by developing strategic capabilities.

Question: In this new working environment, video calls are here to stay. After initially scrambling to get used to them, I notice staff members occasionally slipping into bad habits. Any advice for guidelines I can set?
Answer: The early days of the 2020 pandemic did come with limited guidelines as we figured out how to work from home effectively. There were so many technology issues, so make sure everyone is comfortable with the technology and the platforms they are using. Beyond that, settling into new ways of working means adjusting etiquette and expectations for new formats such as **video calls**. Here are some ideas for you and your staff.

Let's start with a basic guideline, be professional.

- Be groomed and appropriately dressed. It's just common courtesy.
- Mute your mic when you're not speaking.
- Avoid unprofessional actions, like eating, laughing, joking, or smirking during calls. Quirky habits can be amplified on a video conference, especially when all participants are in

full view. Some things that may not be obvious during an in-person meeting when your attention is diverted are now front and center for all to see.

Be present.

- Look at the camera.
- Keep video on so no one can hide out.
- If you must step away during an interactive call, turn your camera off to signal you're temporarily not available.
- If one team member is presenting, everyone goes into speaker view mode and mutes to avoid distraction by other participants. Also, encourage the use of the chat feature for comments and questions, leaving time to address them.
- Use breakout rooms if smaller group conversations are necessary.

Be focused and aware of your surroundings and the nature of the call, especially if people outside your immediate team are on the call. Dedicated workspace in your home can be dressed up or adjusted for video calls, if necessary.

- Adjust the lighting and reduce glare in the background. Having a simple desk lamp in front of you can help.
- Use a background to prevent others from being distracted by views of your home. This also keeps background glare to a minimum.
- Avoid multitasking. It's distracting to others and can negatively affect work quality.

Guidelines can be relaxed at times, especially if the nature of the call is casual or celebratory. The same holds true for in-person meetings.

Question: My organization's annual harassment training has been the same training for years. It's perceived as a check-the-box

requirement, and my team once again complained and raised legitimate issues including changes that have occurred with the workforce and the workplace. I took all these concerns to the leadership, and they asked me to head a taskforce to look for a new training provider. I'm eager to bring a quality program to the employees. What should I be looking for in harassment training?

Answer: Congratulations on your willingness to lead this new initiative to update your organization's **sexual harassment training**. Too often, employers are more concerned about meeting a requirement rather than employees actually learning anything. Training programs that have been around for years are bound to be outdated, and recycling the same tired information only sends a message that the organization does not really take the issue seriously. As you review training providers, here are some things to consider:

- Is the training limited to sexual harassment only? It should address all forms of discrimination and harassment such as race, ethnicity, religion, age, and disability.
- Do discussions of sexual harassment extend beyond issues involving men and women? Even beyond same-sex harassment, it should include discussions about sexual orientation and gender identity—especially harassment against transgender and nonbinary individuals.
- Beyond recognizing harassment, which is the focus of so many training programs, does it provide guidance to employees on what to do if they encounter harassment? Bystander intervention training is a powerful way to encourage employees to speak up, take action, and address the behavior. Such training offers techniques for doing so.
- Does it address working in a hybrid or remote environment and the types of harassment that can occur, such as cyber bullying?
- Is the training appropriate and relevant for your organization and industry? If it's not, ask if they are willing to customize it.
- How do they refresh their training on an annual basis to ensure that it is current and relevant?

Today's workforce, especially the younger members, are savvy and want to contribute to a respectful workplace. As you put your task force together, be sure that it is inclusive and representative of your organization's workforce diversity.

Question: Prior to the pandemic, we used to lighten things up with events and themed lunches and other social activities at work. Much of that is no longer possible with a distributed workforce and new health regulations. Is it still possible to have some fun at work and do you have any ideas for doing so?

Answer: Good for you for thinking of the value of a little **workplace levity.** Life is pretty grim sometimes, so enjoying a moment of fun will go a long way to creating the employee experience you want for your staff.

There are some easy things to do to interject some lightness into a long day, week, or month:

- Open each staff meeting—whether online or in person—with an **ice breaker.** Rotate the "come up with an ice breaker" assignment to your team so you don't have to think of them all. Possible ice breakers include:
  - Share how many kids in your family and where you are in the birth order. (You can keep a tally and share that at the end to see any patterns in your team.)
  - If you won the lottery, what is the first thing you'd do?
  - What is the craziest request you've ever gotten in your career?
  - What is your favorite place to vacation and why?
  - How many states have you visited, and which was your favorite?
  - If you could start a nonprofit, what would it be and why?
  - What is your most embarrassing moment?
  - Who was your teenage celebrity crush? Do you still feel the same way today?

- There is a day for every occasion. Find a day that appeals to your workforce or just sounds like fun, and celebrate that day. For example, January 28 is National Fun at Work Day and April 1 is International Fun at Work Day. You certainly could have some fun celebrating international days by ordering food, or exchanging recipes from different countries or playing trivia about a particular country.
- The internet has many ideas for fun activities for all kinds of situations. Have fun even researching the possibilities.

Most important, if you are serious about having fun at work, get your leaders involved if at all possible. Nothing brings a group together faster than laughing with a high-ranking leader who shares part of themselves that employees haven't seen before. So do your best to involve as many leaders as possible in your fun-at-work exercises.

Question: Communicating with my employees has always been an extremely important part of my job, but now that I manage a hybrid workforce, it is even more critical. Do you have any tips for maintaining good communication skills?

Answer: Effective **communication** with employees is one of the most impactful actions a manager takes. It takes a lot of work but consider the payoff.

When your staff has a clear understanding of organizational and departmental **goals** along with your expectations, great things can happen. Employees will be motivated and more productive when they understand where you're headed. The result: success for your department and organization.

Here are some tips for maintaining your **communication skills:**

- Be as honest and open as possible with your team so they know they are part of something important. Transparency is the key—especially about your expectations. Your employees want to know as much as possible about how your organization is doing even when things aren't going so well.

- Be as approachable as possible with your team and available to them. Let them know they can talk to you about anything and mean it. While there are times when a manager has to be behind a closed door or offline, let your staff know when and how to reach you.
- Be as clear as possible in your message. Think through what you are going to say and be as concise as possible whether you are in person or online. Whenever possible, avoid jargon. If you are sending a written message, use short paragraphs and bullets to clearly communicate your message.
- Be as personal as possible. This includes having individual conversations with each member of your staff as often as you can. A simple *"how are you doing today?"* will have a huge impact on employees. However, ask this question only when you are prepared to listen carefully to the response. If action is needed, don't put it off. Respond as quickly as possible to your employees' needs, such as within twenty-four hours.
- Be a good listener at all times. It will make your employees feel valued. Pay attention to what you hear and take what you hear seriously.

Congratulations for recognizing that communicating with your staff is one of the most important parts of your job. Spend time considering where you can improve your skills and good luck.

Question: I think my listening skills need some improvement in this new environment of hybrid work and video communications. What can I do to be a good listener so I can be the best manager possible?

Answer: Thanks for asking about **listening skills,** an often overlooked but very important part of the communication process. When you show others that you are listening to them, they feel like you respect them.

One of the most effective tools to improve your listening abilities is to learn to use a technique called **active listening**. Using active listening can establish open communication and camaraderie in the workplace.

Here is how it works:

- Whenever possible, limit distractions so that you can focus on what the other person is saying.
- Turn off your listening filters, and don't allow yourself to think of anything except what the other person is saying.
- Use body language to indicate you are hearing what they are saying—a nod or a smile can let them know you are focused on them.
- Beyond body language, use quick phrases, such as *"Yes,"* *"Really?" or "That's interesting,"* to let the other person know you're paying attention.
- Don't start thinking of what you are going to say in response to what they are saying until they have finished their thought.
- Summarize what the speaker is saying. Say something like, *"What I heard you say was . . ."* This gives the speaker an opportunity to clarify any points they made that you heard differently from what they meant.
- Ask follow-up questions to show you are invested in the conversation. For example, *"Tell me more" or "How so?"* Ask questions that will allow them to give you more information or elaborate on their main points.

Active listening is one of many techniques you can use to be a better listener. Consider taking a class, or find a mentor who can help you improve your listening skills. You will be glad you did.

Question: Some leaders in my organization think that the employees who work in the office are more productive than those who work remotely or from home. Can you give me some information to help dispel their theories?

Answer: Leaders who feel this way are likely expressing personal beliefs and not using facts, and it's hard to change people's minds. However, if you're looking for facts about the productivity of remote workers, there is lots of data supporting the point that **remote workers** can be highly productive.

When evaluating whether your employees are more productive in the office or at home, look at individuals and not large groups of people. **Productivity** for remote workers depends on having the right tools to do the job, the proper level of self-motivation, and innovative and flexible supervision.

Get your leaders to spell out where they are coming from so you can respond to their concerns. Start by defining productivity, which usually means how efficient an employee is in completing a specific task. Tie productivity to effectiveness which can be further defined as the *capability of producing a desired result*. Do these definitions work for your leaders, or are they defining productivity in terms of profitability: how much we made this year versus last year?

Trying to figure out the world of work while actually doing the work isn't easy to do. There is no surprise that some people aren't comfortable working with coworkers they don't physically see daily, and we may not ever totally return to that model.

In fact, we've been moving away from that way of working for a long time. Consider how many organizations have long operated globally with employees on different continents, led by people most employees never met and probably never will meet. **Global teams** have operated the same way. Has that stopped them from being productive?

Thanks to highly usable technology, employees can chat with anyone at any time with less effort than getting out of their office chairs and visiting a coworker down the hall, provided staff members are equipped with the tools to do their jobs from wherever they sit.

As you navigate this murky issue of who is more productive, remote versus in-office staff, recognize there isn't a one-size-fits-all model. Focus on helping your leaders do their best to inspire, motivate, and reward your great employees for their contributions—no matter where they physically work. We wish you well.

Question: I keep hearing talk of something called employee well-being and how important it has become to today's workforce. What is employee well-being, and is this just another word for wellness?

Answer: It is easy to be confused by these two terms, but they are different. **Employee well-being** is ensuring that staff are treated with care, compassion, and trust. Wellness may be a component of well-being, but it usually focuses on activities such as exercise, yoga, weight loss, smoking cessation programs, and similar activities.

Smart managers know that team members today want to be treated like a human being and not just an employee. They want to know their manager and their leadership value them for more than the work they produce for the organization.

This concept can be difficult for some managers who want to stay as far as possible from their staff members. They are finding that ways of interacting (or not interacting) with employees can have a negative impact on productivity and engagement.

Don't ignore the **wellness programs** that have surfaced in recent years—more on this in Section 3—but think in broader terms about the well-being of your team. For example:

- Sincerely ask each team member how they are and really listen to their answer. If your staff is remote or hybrid, call them personally and ask how they are. You will be amazed at the response you will get. Be sure to take action where you can, so your next call will be as productive.
- Keep your word. Trust is a huge component of well-being. If your team doesn't trust you because you don't back them up or you don't do what you say you will do, that trust will be broken, and it is hard to get it back.
- Find ways to encourage people to take time off to recharge. Consider instituting no meeting Fridays and setting a policy

where emails are not required to be answered during certain hours and on weekends. Show your employees you value them by encouraging them to take time away from their jobs— vacation or an occasional long weekend, or hours off during the workday.

- Check with your leadership to ensure your organization's benefits program has strong coverage, especially in the area of mental health.

If your employees feel you genuinely care about them as a human being and trust you, their well-being will be strong, and you will be viewed as a trusted manager. Give it a try.

Question: Resolving conflicts between staff members was challenging enough when we were all working in the same place. With our new working arrangements—people in the office, people at home, others in remote locations—conflict hasn't been eliminated. We meet as often as possible using technology. Any suggestions on how I can resolve issues when they arise with this distributed workforce?

Answer: It would have been great if one of the benefits of a **distributed workforce** was that we had peace and harmony all the time. However, there will always be differences in attitudes and work styles whether we work side by side or only see each other online.

Wherever your team is working, you can take proactive steps to minimize **conflict**.

- Set clear expectations. Be sure staff members know their goals and what they need to deliver and by when. Reiterate this, frequently if necessary, so that you are sure you're all on the same page.
- Make sure your job descriptions are up to date so that people are clear about their role and their responsibilities. Conflict often happens because people aren't sure where their job ends

and their coworker's start. Current job descriptions can help avoid confusion.

- Sharpen your listening and observing skills. Communicating online is challenging. It's easy to miss physical cues you'd easily see if you were in person, but with concentration, you can get better at observing body language online. Watch for eye rolls, smirks, and frowns as people are speaking. You may be observing conflicts or the beginnings of conflicts that you may be able to head off.

Emphasize to your employees you need to be alerted when issues do come up between them. No matter if you are all in one place or not, if you aren't aware of an issue, you have no hope of addressing it. Let your team know you want to hear from them when they are unhappy about something or someone so you can help them resolve the issue.

When you are made aware of a conflict, schedule individual time with each person involved to get their side of the story, letting each know you are speaking to the other person or people. Gather any relevant facts or observations of others, if appropriate. Then meet again, collectively, online to work out a solution.

While working virtually may complicate the process, listening carefully and using your powers of observation will lead to creative problem solving and solutions. If not, you may need to counsel the people involved or take other steps to address their behavior.

Question: The HR department at my organization is doing a great job helping with the many challenges my staff members are facing, especially in these changing times. Unfortunately, I don't think my staff is aware of all the resources HR has available for them. Other than suggesting they make good use of those resources, do you have any ideas of how I can encourage them to learn more about, and use, these resources?

Answer: Good for you for recognizing the contributions being made by your **HR department**. We wish more people would acknowledge the impact HR makes on successful organizations.

Yes, you can do more than just make suggestions. The best place to start is modeling the behavior you want your staff to emulate. Bring HR team members to your staff meetings, whether in person or virtually. Ask them to share what they are working on. Work with HR to prepare a resource list for your employees that provides them with information sources your team may not be aware of.

Ask members of the HR team to do webinars for your staff on topics you know would be helpful for your team—available benefits or training programs are two examples. This, of course, means you know the HR team and know what they can bring to your staff. Inviting them to talk with your team will strengthen your relationship with HR and help them learn more about what your department does and where you and the team members are challenged.

Whenever possible, say complimentary things about your interactions with HR. Share how they've helped you and other leaders in your organization tackle some of the most difficult situations in our new normal. When your team members ask you for information that you know HR has readily available, refer your employee to HR, then ask the team member to share their experience with HR and the information they received, if appropriate, at you next staff meeting.

HR departments are making major impacts, and it would be a shame for your team not to take advantage of what they have to offer.

Question: In our new hybrid world at work, I miss seeing my team in person as often as I used to. We had a great team spirit, and it is a bit harder to do that now. I am willing to try new ideas and make changes to how we communicate, but I need a little help on how I can let my employees know how much I value them. Any ideas?

Answer: Thank you for asking this question, which is at or near the heart of creating a positive employee experience. There are things you can do to maintain **team spirit** even in a **hybrid work** arrangement so your team knows how you value them, such as:

- Telling them often that you value them as human beings but only if you mean it and if your actions support your words. We have mentioned the importance of trust in a few answers in this book. We've shared that one of the ways managers build trust with their staff members is by always being honest.
- Asking them for ideas and suggestions when it is appropriate. Don't just ask for suggestions and move on. Whenever possible, use their ideas and give the employee who brought it forward the credit.
- Acknowledging team accomplishments. For example, when you reach a milestone on a project or surpass expectations, celebrate as a team. If it's possible, this might be an excellent time to get everyone into the office at the same time for a special meeting.
- Rewarding extra effort with a thank you or something more tangible such as a day off with pay or a gift card to a local restaurant. Keep in mind that some people do not like to be rewarded in public, so be sure you understand what would be motivating for that particular person.
- Facilitating development opportunities by assigning employees to task forces or to serve on highly visible projects.

There are many more ways to show employees you value them. See what you think will work for your staff, and you are sure to see results.

AVOIDING LEGAL PITFALLS

Question: When I hear about sexual harassment, I think of unwanted physical contact, invasion of personal space, or staring or leering at someone. Now I'm hearing that online interactions are being described as harassment or bullying. I'm confused. Can

you shed some light on this along with advice for handling these
situations?

Answer: Unfortunately, in today's virtual environment, people
are becoming emboldened and finding new ways to misbehave. One
employee was mortified when a manager sang her a love song during
a zoom meeting. **Microaggressions,** making sexual comments,
remarks, or jokes, sharing or circulating suggestive images and
threatening messages, are all examples of behavior that is likely **sexual harassment** or bullying. All of these behaviors can take place via
video calls, text messages, and emails. People who tend to be polite in
face-to-face conversation can have a completely different personality
when they're hidden behind a screen or keyboard.

Whether the behavior is occurring in person or virtually, as a
manager you should always be proactive.

- Talk about disruptive behavior of all types in meetings
  with your staff. Let them know that such behavior won't be
  tolerated.
- Have open conversations about the organization's policies with
  individual employees and in staff meetings. Listen to their
  concerns.
- Encourage your employees to discuss with you any behavior
  they feel is inappropriate. Less severe behavior can quickly
  erode into harassment or worse if not addressed.
- Let your team know that they are empowered to report harassment and discrimination to you, legal or human resources
  without fear of retaliation.
- If you hear or suspect that the policies and practices your organization has in place are not working, let your senior leaders
  know so it can be determined why they aren't working.
- Don't ignore comments or behavior that's reported to you or
  that you observe. Confront and act on them in accordance
  with your organization's policies and support any necessary
  corrective action.

Being proactive and taking action when disruptive behavior occurs not only maintains the organization's positive culture, it also builds your personal trust and credibility. Your employees will have confidence in you and the organization and be proud to be a part of it.

Question: With so many employees working from home, I assume that those with disabilities likely do not have as many barriers. What is the extent of employers' obligations to provide reasonable accommodations?

Answer: You're correct that remote work does remove many of the physical accessibility barriers for individuals with disabilities, along with the challenges of transportation. **Telework**, in fact, has long been considered a **reasonable accommodation**. It has provided employees with disabilities the flexibility to customize their workspaces, schedules, and any other medical or medication management.

However, none of this means that employers don't have an obligation to provide reasonable accommodations under the **Americans with Disabilities Act (ADA)**. Consider the amount of video conferencing and meetings that are conducted today. This can have an impact on individuals with sensory disabilities—hearing or visual impairments. For example, someone with a hearing disability may struggle accessing video calls. Individuals with sensory impairments may need some type of assistive technology, such as voice recognition programs, screen readers, screen enlargement applications, or closed captioning.

A **reasonable accommodation** removes unnecessary barriers that prevent or restrict employment opportunities and enables a qualified individual with a disability to perform the essential functions of the job. A word of caution: The accommodation must be tailored to the individual employee's needs. There is not a one-size-fits-all accommodation that will work for every visual impairment, for instance. It's for that reason that the **Equal Employment Opportunity Commission**, in its ADA guidance, recommends an interactive process between employees (and applicants) and the employer to determine the most effective accommodation.

There are a number of sources available for consultation. The Job Accommodation Network (askjan.org) is a government-funded resource. Employers can contact a JAN counselor who can perform an individualized search for a workplace accommodation based on the job requirements and the employee's needs. This is an excellent place to start. Also don't overlook your state's vocational rehabilitation program. Remember, the most important thing is to keep the individual involved in the process.

Question: It sounds like legal requirements don't necessarily go away just because people are working from home. What else do managers like me need to be aware of?

Answer: You're absolutely right. Legal obligations follow employers no matter where their employees work. Having employees in various locations can make the challenges greater. These are some requirements you should be aware of:

- **The Fair Labor Standards Act,** especially the overtime requirements. We've included a question on this topic in Section 3, Paying and Rewarding Employees.
- **Workers Compensation,** especially ergonomics. A question about this can be found in Section 5, Understanding Policies and Practices.
- **The Family and Medical Leave Act.** You can't assume that because an employee is working from home, they don't need time away from work duties to care for a sick family member or a newborn or newly adopted child.

In addition to **sexual harassment,** which is discussed above, there are other areas of discrimination (yes, sexual harassment is form a of discrimination) that managers and employers need to be mindful of when managing a **remote workforce or hybrid workforce.**

- If employees have a choice between working at home or working in the office, are the decisions being made fairly and without bias? As long as the work can be performed from home, are all employees given the same advantage to work from home?
- Are the employees who work in the office being given **preferential treatment** over those who do not? For example, are they being given better assignments, or are they receiving more frequent feedback? This can be a potential problem, especially if the majority of individuals working from home are people of color or members of other protected groups. They may be missing out on opportunities that could enhance career growth.
- If a large number of employees working from home are, in fact, people of color, are they doing so in order to avoid **microaggressions**? It's worth taking the time to inquire because it could be an indicator of a greater problem with your culture, in addition to possible discrimination.

If you discover any indicators of potential problems, be sure to bring them to the attention of your management team, including HR and legal advisors, so they can be addressed and corrected.

CLOSING THOUGHTS

While the term *Employee Experience* may be relatively new, what it involves has been around for a long time. It is basically a way to name the concept of how you treat your employees, which makes a huge difference in how they feel about their jobs. It may sound simplistic, but happy and engaged employees are more productive. So why wouldn't you want them to feel good about where they work and what they do on a daily basis? Working to ensure your staff has a positive experience is a good thing.

SECTION 3

PAYING AND REWARDING EMPLOYEES

WHILE PAY IS not the primary reason your employees come to work every day, it is near the top of the list. Therefore, paying people fairly and, of course, in a timely fashion, is significantly important. However, there are a lot of moving parts to compensation. You have to be sure you are competitive in your marketplace, and you need to be sure your pay structure fits into your organization's budgeting process and philosophy. Virtual work has further complicated how you pay, and then there's the looming issue of pay transparency.

This section provides some technical assistance for you so that your organization's compensation programs meet your needs. We also look at benefits and nonmonetary related rewards.

Question: I've been told that my organization has a compensation philosophy that says we will meet the market. HR explained in a meeting that our jobs are matched to the 50th percentile of market data. I'm confused. Does this mean we are only being paid half of what our jobs are worth in the market?

Answer: Discussions about compensation, like any technical area, can be confusing. Let's break this down. When an organization's

compensation philosophy is to meet or match the market, it means that it will pay the going rate for its jobs in the market in which it operates.

The labor market has to be determined before salary data can be gathered. Considerations include the geographic areas where the jobs are located and the organization's industry. Once the labor market is determined, organizations will typically consult external salary surveys—tools used to determine the median or the average salaries paid to employees. There are many reputable providers of salary surveys, and your organization is likely using data from them. These providers collect pay data from several employers and then analyze it to determine the salary or compensation paid for each job. In fact, your organization may even participate in one or more of these surveys. Jobs are usually matched by comparing job duties rather than job titles since different titles mean different things in different organizations.

In compensation speak, quartiles and percentiles are commonly recognized reference points used to measure an organization's position against the market, that is if they lead, lag, or match a particular labor market. They also show the dispersion within a **salary range** and help in determining internal compensation equity. The 50th percentile, or the midpoint, generally represents the average pay for the individual positions in the survey. That's the benchmark in the market data to which HR is referring—the benchmark for meeting the average pay in the market. If your organization's philosophy was to lead the market, they would be comparing positions and pay at a higher level than the average pay, likely against the 75th percentile or 25 percent higher than the average. Conversely, if the philosophy was to lag, the benchmark would be the 25th percentile, or 25 percent lower than the average.

It would be a good idea to ask to meet with HR so they can discuss this with you in further detail. Having clarity around compensation issues will allow you to have more meaningful discussions with your team members.

Question: We have a difficult topic involving hiring salaries for candidates we really want to hire. Is there anything we can do when a well-qualified candidate asks for more money than we are prepared to pay using our established salary ranges as a guide?

Answer: This is an all-too-common occurrence as pay information is shared on sites like PayScale and Glassdoor and yes, there is something you can do.

Let's say your **compensation philosophy** is to meet the market, so you offer an applicant $90,000 plus benefits. This is a number that fits into your **salary ranges**—between the minimum and the midpoint of the range. But the candidate says they are looking for $100,000, and almost everyone negotiates on salary now.

One option to consider is to offer the candidate a one-time **hiring bonus** of $10,000. Some of you may balk at a hiring bonus—after all, they haven't contributed anything to your success yet.

However, there are some things to consider about a hiring bonus that may make this work for even the skeptics.

A hiring bonus is a one-time payment. It doesn't inflate the employee's salary, and future increases will be made on their base salary of $90,000. A hiring bonus doesn't impact your organization's internal equity—what you pay current employees in that salary range.

The offer of a hiring bonus can make a big difference to the candidate and may seal the deal.

There is a possible negative to the hiring bonus for the new hire. Since it is a one-time occurrence, there may be a let down for them in their second year. Hopefully, their performance will be at a level where they will receive a good increase, or they could be promoted into a higher range. Just don't lose sight of this possibility.

Something else to keep in mind: When was the last time your **salary ranges** were adjusted to ensure you are as competitive as possible? If they haven't been adjusted in a while, it's time to consider it and talk with the leadership and HR about it. While you're at it, look at your benefits package and other things you offer to new hires just to be sure you are as competitive as possible.

Question: An employee just came to me claiming they were being underpaid and asking for a raise. To prove their point, they cited salaries for positions similar to theirs that they saw on Glassdoor. Are these sources reliable and should I be concerned?

Answer: As we said in the last question, this is an all-too-common occurrence as pay information is shared on sites like Glassdoor or other social media platforms. As **pay transparency** becomes more common, and as more organizations are required to include salary data in job postings, questions like the one your employee posed are likely to occur more frequently.

Let's begin by looking at the source of the information the employee is citing. Information from platforms such as Glassdoor rely on **crowdsourced data** which is employee-reported data—data that can be inflated. There is no way to verify its accuracy. Other concerns with this data that need to be considered: 1) there is inherent bias since the participants self-select in; and 2) job titles alone can be meaningless—there is no consideration of job scope and duties, or the industry, as examples.

Other available salary data that is widely available is data contained in job listings, such as those found on platforms like LinkedIn. This is referred to as scraped data.

Compensation experts rely more heavily on traditional salary survey data because it's based on proven methodologies, trusted relationships, and established data. Salary survey data is reliable, credible, and more accurate. For example, in traditional **salary surveys**, job titles alone are not compared. Rather, they rely on job descriptions—descriptions of basic duties—which are better comparators.

Of course, in these rapidly changing times, traditional data sources may not keep up with emerging jobs and skills, can be dated or aged, and may lag the market. That's when the experts turn to crowdsourced and/or scraped data. These sources might be used as supplemental data—a data-point in overall market assessment, or in pricing one job, especially if it's a newly emerging position.

Have a discussion with your HR team about the employee's inquiry. They should be able to give you some guidance on responding that reflects your organization's compensation system. Perhaps it's time for a managers' briefing on compensation.

Question: I am hearing a lot about pay transparency, and you referred to it in the last question. What is it, and do we have to be concerned or do something with it?

Answer: You're right. This is becoming an increasingly hot topic and practice. And yes, you should pay some attention to it.

What is it? **Pay transparency** is what the title says—the organization is open about its pay philosophy and salary ranges. It is a way of opening up what has been "secret" information. Many states have passed laws regarding pay transparency, and the trend is rapidly growing.

A previous question discussed having a **compensation philosophy**. A compensation philosophy can help with the issue of transparency. It will give you a frame of reference when you are discussing pay with new hires or when you are negotiating a salary increase with a current employee.

Salary information has been a carefully guarded secret for most organizations, but it is becoming increasingly obvious that employees want to know how their organization pays its people. Is there some sort of system or are decisions made randomly?

A transparent **pay system** can go a long way toward building trust with your employees. Let your staff know that you do salary surveys to compare your salaries to others in your industry. Share your salary grades openly so employees can see what jobs are in a higher grade that they might aspire to.

Organizations that practice pay transparency have found that it positively impacts their bottom line, creates a cohesive workforce, and minimizes distractions. Studies have found that when pay is secret, people frequently overestimate their coworkers' pay, which has a negative impact on their **job satisfaction**. And, including pay ranges in job postings can increase applications for open positions— especially female and minority applicants.

With the rapid growth in online sharing of information, pay transparency is most likely going to stay with us. Discuss it with your leadership, including HR. Think positively—it is actually good news for organizations and for job seekers.

Implementing a practice of pay transparency requires a well- thought-out **compensation system** and comprehensive manage- ment training. Managers are on the front line and will be the ones responding to the questions employees ask, so they need the tools to make this a positive experience for everyone.

Question: Pay transparency is fine, and I understand what you said in the last question. However, an employee just confronted me claiming she learned another employee is making more money than she does. He clearly has more and varied experience. She was very angry and emotional, hinting at discrimination. I'd like her to develop her skills, but I'm not sure how to address this issue. What would you suggest?

Answer: These conversations are always difficult, so take a deep breath and don't get overwhelmed. For starters, let's assume that the differences in their salaries are justified within your compensation sys- tem. To be safe, let your HR and legal team know about her concerns.

It looks like you have three issues here, so let's start with her **emo- tional behavior**. Acknowledge her emotions and express under- standing that the situation might be upsetting to her. However, it's important to let her know that her anger is not productive and will interfere with your discussions. Remain calm and objective as you begin to relate the facts underlying the situation.

From there, you need to move on to describe how individual employee's compensation is determined. Explain that while she and her coworker may have the same job title, that there are variances. In this case, his years of experience is clearly a factor. Perhaps, for example, his varied experience gives him the opportunity to take on more complex assignments or enables him to work more independently. Be prepared to discuss what differentiates his background from hers and how these differences factor into his higher salary.

Finally, use the opportunity to let her know that she is a valuable member of the team and that you want to develop her skills further so she will be able to assume more complex and varied responsibilities. This is an excellent opportunity to start the conversation regarding an **individual development plan** for her. Get her input regarding her career goals and have some developmental opportunities in mind to share with her.

Question: An employee recently asked for a significant raise, in the 15 to 20 percent range. They presented examples of their work accomplishment, and I agree their performance is very good. However, they mentioned personal financial hardships they were experiencing as justification for the increase. Their current salary is in line with their coworkers. Without sounding cold hearted, how do I explain that a 15 percent increase is way above the norm and that we can't grant a raise based on an individual's need?

Answer: One reason organizations have been criticized over compensation is because employees see it from their individual viewpoint and needs without considering others in the same job. This is where **compensation transparency** can assist.

Meet with the employee and discuss their current salary. Show them the **salary range** for their job and explain where their individual salary fits in that range. If it's comparable or higher to others, mention that without disclosing the individual salaries of coworkers.

Talk to the employee about the annual **salary budget** that you and all managers have to work with. Explain that this budget has to be allocated across the department and the organization. If you gave them more—and yes, a 15 to 20 percent increase for doing their current job does sound unreasonable—it would mean that others doing equally good work would receive less, and that is not fair.

After laying this foundation, explain how compensation is determined. Employers base compensation for each job on the value the job brings to the organization. They look at variables in the overall labor market, such as what other organizations in the same industry are paying for the same jobs.

Beyond that, employers set individual salaries based on factors such as experience and performance. When determining what to pay someone, the individual's financial situation is not a factor in that decision. Without suggesting that this employee made bad decisions that caused their financial hardships, ask if they think it would be fair if someone doing equally good work was paid less because they didn't have the same financial needs.

Keep your discussion with the employee focused and based on facts. Consider discussing promotional opportunities and how you can support their development. This will give them a potential path forward in your organization. Ultimately, however, the employee will have to make a decision that's best for them and their family.

Question: I have an employee whose salary is at the top of the salary range for their position. They are a valued contributor in a somewhat unique role and not interested in a promotion. I'm told I can't give them a raise, but I want to reward them. Is there a downside to simply ignoring the fact that their salary has reached its limit and trying to push through a raise?

Answer: I'm glad that you realize it's important to reward and recognize valued contributors who are on your team. You'd be surprised at how many managers simply ignore the fact that someone has reached the **top of the salary range** and try to push a raise through as you suggest. However, that's not the answer. Salary ranges are not set arbitrarily. A significant amount of work, research, and analysis goes into developing them.

It's time to check with your HR team and discuss several possibilities.

- Salary structures are not static and are often adjusted to reflect changes in the job market. If there are no plans to do so in time for the next merit increase cycle, it's possible it may occur next year. This will give you a sense of timing and help you plan a strategy.
- If the position your employee holds is that unique, the salary survey data that was used to place the job in its range may be outdated. Inquire whether supplemental data could be used.
- Talk with human resources about doing a job study to determine if the employee's position is properly classified and in the appropriate salary grade. You indicated that their role is unique. Is it possible that new and varied responsibilities have been added since the job was originally placed into the current salary range? Just as salary ranges are adjusted over time, so are job classifications.

If there are no immediate plans to look at position classifications, salaries, or salary ranges, consider giving the employee a one-time bonus this year, perhaps equal to the amount of what their merit increase would have been. This strategy maintains their base salary within the salary range of their position, while at the same time rewarding them for excellent work.

Question: I was recently interviewing a candidate for an open position when they brought up salary. I asked them what they were currently making and got pushback. How do I make a salary recommendation to HR if I don't know what someone's salary expectation is?

Answer: I see more than one issue in your question. The first, and most important, is making a **salary** recommendation. Salaries are based on the **value of the position** to the organization. As mentioned in earlier questions in this section, HR conducts studies to set salary structures and market competitiveness. An individual candidate's current salary should not be a factor for a number of reasons. For example:

1. They might be working in a different industry (nonprofit, for example) where their current employer's labor costs may vary from your organizations.
2. They may be embarking on a career change moving from a higher paying position to a lower paying one, which has significant growth potential. In such a case, their current salary may not be an indicator of their expected salary in a new field.
3. They may have been undervalued or underpaid by their current employer.

The second issue is that a number of cities and states have **pay history question bans** where employers are banned from asking applicants about salary histories. One of the reasons for this ban is tied to number three in the previous list. Looking at the history of **equal pay** and **salary equity**, one reason frequently cited that may have contributed to women being paid lower than men is that men are better negotiators. (Of course, this is likely only one of many factors.)

Complicating the second issue is our current state of remote and hybrid work. If the organization is located in one state, but the applicant lives and *will likely work* in another, the question arises: Which jurisdiction and laws take precedent? Clearly, your HR and legal teams can provide guidance here.

Legal requirements aside, a best practice is to avoid discussing a candidate's current salary. If they ask about salary, provide a salary range. When you've selected the best candidate for the job, work with HR and your organization's salary structure when determining the salary to offer.

Question: An employee I recently hired who started working a few weeks ago asked for time off to attend a family member's destination wedding. They haven't accrued sufficient paid time off (PTO)

to cover the time. I'm concerned if I agree to let them have the time off that I'll be setting a precedent. What do you think?

Response: A couple of things come to mind reading your question. The first is the very broad and important issue that cannot be ignored: recognizing that employees do have lives away from work, and work does not and should not encompass their entire lives.

With that in mind, we have seen organizations get anxious over this issue because they don't want to set a **precedent**. However, what precedent, exactly, are you concerned about setting. What, exactly, has the employee asked for? Simply the time off to attend the event, time off and to use the limited leave they've accrued, or time off with the expectation that it will all be paid?

If the employee is expecting to take the time off with full pay without sufficient **PTO** to cover the time, your concern in granting that request is valid. Unless you have a generous policy of advancing paid leave under these circumstances, you could be setting a precedent that you'd have difficulty meeting in the future.

On the other hand, absent a restrictive policy about taking time off—paid or unpaid—without sufficient accrued leave, what's the harmful precedent if the employee is asking for either the first or second choice. If your policy is that restrictive, what would you do if the employee were ill? Would you restrict their ability to take time off? If so, what message are you sending about your organization and its culture? With that in mind, consider how much time and effort you put into recruiting and hiring this employee. If the time off is denied, they are likely to start looking for another job, and soon.

NAVIGATING THE CHANGING WORKPLACE

Question: I've read that because of the increase in employees working from remote locations, some organizations have implemented pay cuts for these workers. This doesn't seem fair. Do you have any ideas on why employers would want to decrease pay or prevent employees from moving?

Answer: Once office space began reopening after the pandemic, there were some organizations who announced across-the-board pay cuts for employees who wanted to **voluntarily relocate** to other geographic locations and continue working remotely. Many of these relocations were from large metropolitan areas to more remote and less densely populated areas.

This practice of adjusting pay is called **pay localization,** a practice in which workers pay is based on cost of living and/or cost of labor in a particular geographic location. In developing compensation systems and setting rates of pay, geographic location has typically been one of the many variables taken into consideration.

A different approach some organizations take is **salary portability.** In this method, when the employee moves to a location where a benchmark for compensation has not been set up, the employer considers the local pay rates of the new locale, but it also combines those figures with the employer's own compensation survey data and internal benchmarks for a given role to determine how employees should be paid in a given part of the country.

As a manager, if you have an employee considering a voluntary relocation, it's important to keep several things in mind as you consult with your leadership team. Beyond how compensation will be set, your organization will have to research and comply with state and local laws and regulations, including wage and hour laws. There are tax considerations, for the employer and the employee, as well. For example, in addition to payroll tax withholdings, the employer may be required to file income tax returns if the employee moves to a location where the organization has no other presence or business.

Keep in mind that if employers resist an employee's remote move, it may be because they don't have sufficient resources to manage all the issues associated with a highly distributed workforce.

Question: I'm a firm believer in exercise. When all my staff was in the office every day, I made it a point to have walking meetings once a week. It kept people moving and energized. Now that we've moved

to a hybrid work arrangement and the staff is rarely together in the office, I'm looking for ideas to keep them moving. Any thoughts on virtual exercise programs, apps, or other things I can do to keep them moving and active?

Answer: Kudos for thinking of your staff and their well-being. **Employee wellness** is so important, especially with remote workers and hybrid work arrangements.

There are a number of on-demand fitness options and platforms, and many organizations are purchasing memberships and subscriptions to them for their employees as an alternative to gym memberships. If this doesn't fit your needs, there are other things and activities you can consider.

- Challenge employees to get in a certain number of steps a day. This can include taking short walking breaks (in lieu of your walking meetings) or just walking around their homes or buildings. Either way, they get their steps in. Offer prizes to make it competitive.
- Add to the idea of a step challenge by encouraging team members to do 10 to 15 minutes of cardio exercises each day. If they are working from home, they can take advantage of equipment they may have at their disposal.
- Have a team member lead short exercise sessions—five to ten minutes in length. For example, yogis can show off simple yoga poses and have everyone participate. You can also have everyone do stretches for ten to fifteen minutes.
- Do a messy desk clean-up challenge that involves giving everyone a time frame—fifteen minutes for example—to tidy up their desk or workspace. To get them moving, make it a requirement that they stand while doing so. Turn it into a contest, and have the team vote on the most impressive makeover.

There are other components to **virtual wellness** that you should not be overlooking. Offer nutrition resources and have healthy cooking and eating challenges; or introduce meditation and relaxation programs, including mindfulness. The goal is to encourage healthier lifestyles, especially if the nature of the work is sedentary.

Question: So much is being written about employee burnout. Beyond my team members physical well-being, I'm also concerned by their overall well-being, such as mental health and financial wellness. As a manager, what can I be doing in these areas?

Answer: Committing to your employees' overall well-being is something every organization should be doing. Some things, like benefit offerings, are decided at a leadership level. Managers, however, have a great deal of influence.

Start with setting explicit boundaries to avoid a culture where the expectation is you have to be "always on." More importantly, live and exemplify those boundaries. Employees always follow the manager's lead. Some simple steps will go a long way to address **employee burnout** and **mental health**.

- If your organization is large enough, consider setting servers so they don't route emails between certain hours (e.g. 6 p.m. to 7 a.m.). If you can't do this, then set the expectation with your team and then adhere to it.
- Stress that not only evenings, but weekends, are personal time. Set the expectation that no work-related activities should take place.
- Have Zoom-free or no meeting Fridays (or any other day).

Recognize that a little empathy and trust goes a long way.

- Ask employees how they are doing; how their families are doing. This is different from asking about how the project or the work is progressing.
- Employers are paying more attention to the **financial wellness** of their employees. Whether or not your organization can

afford to offer benefits in these areas, as a manager, be mindful that if employees are having financial difficulties, those difficulties may be the cause of some stress.

- If you become aware that employees are stressed over finances or other life situations, encourage them to use the **employee assistance program**. Cut them some slack as well.
- **DEI (diversity, equity, and inclusion)** and social justice issues are very real to today's workforce. Take them seriously, listen to your employee's concerns, and participate in your organization's DEI efforts.
- Encourage employees to use their **paid time off** so they can recharge. Be sure you model the behavior by taking time off yourself.

Question: Almost every day I see an article or blog on the 4-day workweek. Is this something we need to be paying attention to or is it a *passing fancy*?

Answer: You're right. There is a lot of media attention being paid to this idea, but it appears it does not yet have wide acceptance in the business community.

That said, please don't ignore the issues being raised by the suggestion of a **four-day workweek**. One of the primary reasons for shortening the workweek is to avoid burnout. While cutting a day from the workweek may not be the strategy you select to keep your employees from burnout, you should be aware of what you can do for their sanity.

Consider ideas like fewer meetings, or no meetings Fridays, or more **asynchronous work** which we discuss in Section 2. Something else that may help is to give teams more flexibility to break down their projects into more manageable tasks. Also, look at the suggestions in the prior two questions about **employees' mental, emotional, and physical wellness**.

Maybe it is time for your organization to look at how work is assigned and how it is managed. Doesn't what really matter is what the outcome of the effort produces? Aren't you looking for results and productivity?

Consider if there are ways or available technology that can get you the results you're seeking that also may give your employees some of their personal time back. That's one of the arguments in favor of the four-day workweek. Nevertheless, one thing that has to be eliminated is the bragging rights some people feel are important—the attitude: *I worked seventy hours last week, what about you?*

Keep your eye on this idea while you monitor productivity and burnout of your staff. If you want to give the four-day workweek a try, do a trial run in your organization and carefully monitor the results. If this concept catches on with your competitors, you may want to revisit it, but only for the right reasons. Looks like you will have time to make a good decision for your organization since the bandwagon hasn't left yet.

Question: I understand how important it is to recognize and reward my employees and show appreciation for their hard work. Now that we spend more time apart than together, I am not sure what to do nor how to do it. I want to reward them appropriately so that they will continue to produce excellent results. Any thoughts?

Answer: You have hit on a very important part of a manager's job—**recognizing and rewarding** your team. Unfortunately, it is a bit more complicated than when more of us were working in the same location. However, organizations have been working in multiple locations for a long time, so we can learn from past practices while being a bit more creative.

Let's look at some ideas:

- Staff working remotely may feel isolated from the rest of the team, with most interaction occurring between the manager and the employee. To meet this challenge, organize online chats, meeting with your entire team as often as possible online. Encourage your team to create social media groups where they can get to know each other and share ideas.

- Use your online meetings to acknowledge great performance. Create an award that is given out for a special achievement. If the winner is a remote worker, mail or deliver the award to their home and have them open it on camera in a staff meeting. No matter what, don't overlook any chance to acknowledge work that goes above and beyond.

- Send written notes to thank employees for achieving a significant accomplishment, and include a gift card to a local restaurant or to an online shopping site that anyone can use. Here's where it pays to know your employees. If you know a staff member has a particular hobby, send a gift card they can use to indulge that passion. If an employee is a pet lover, give them an online gift certificate to a pet store or site. Be as creative as possible and watch the smiles light up.

- Keep the traditions you had in the past, like celebrating birthdays or work anniversaries. Consider having a monthly video conference where all birthdays for that month are celebrated. If the recipients are remote, have a cake delivered to their home in time for them to be on camera.

Remote appreciation begins with awareness and thoughtfulness. Spend some time thinking about your team and how to recognize their contributions to your organization's success. Turn that appreciation into **tangible rewards** that your staff will enjoy and that acknowledges you value them as a staff member, and as a person.

Question: Before the pandemic, we offered a number of benefits that were tied to working in the office. These included subsidized commuting costs, free snacks, and frequent catered lunches. Naturally, this has all changed. Now that we are settled into a hybrid model, employees are asking whether we plan to bring some

of these benefits back. **What do we tell them, and do you have any ideas about different benefits we can offer?**

Answer: Any change is hard especially if it's accompanied by the perception that something is being lost. You can begin by explaining the rationale for not bringing back some of the **perks** that employees enjoyed in the past. Here are some reasons that you can share:

- Working from home provides employees with reduced commuting costs accompanied by reduced costs for wardrobe and lunches out.
- Employees have also gained additional time (no commute) and flexibility, giving them additional time for personal and family responsibility.
- Many organizations are doing away with communal food situations—kitchens, snacks, catered lunches—for health and safety reasons post-pandemic.
- With less employees in the office, the organization is not able to take advantage of bulk buying discounts for the snacks.

Now, what can you do to offset some of these changes?

During the pandemic, some organizations offered **stipends** to cover employees' increased utility costs at home. Since you were subsidizing commuting costs in the past, is it possible to offer all employees a monthly stipend, which they can use to offset either commuting or utility costs or the costs of eating lunch at home?

If your firm still has occasional catered lunches, consider having individually wrapped choices rather than platters with unwrapped sandwiches for example, to enforce your commitment to a healthy workplace.

Finally consider surveying your workforce to see what types of **benefits** they would like to have. Of course, you can't offer everything. However, some organizations have gotten creative, especially if a number of employees request something specific. For example, you could negotiate reduced rates for veterinary care or pet day care if enough employees want it. The employees would still pay for the benefit, but they would be paying less. These creative ideas can be a win for everyone.

Question: One of our employees has asked to move several hundreds of miles from our office. Our workplace is almost totally virtual, but this particular employee needs to spend time each week in the general vicinity of our office. This is a highly valued staff member whom we do not want to lose. What is a good way to compensate them for trips to the office each week?

Answer: Let's start with the key factor in your question. The move to a new location that is away from your office is entirely the idea of the employee. Right?

If you'd requested the employee to move to a new location, you would pay the expenses of the employee for travel to and from the new location. That is common sense, but also a good business practice.

However, since the move is at the employee's request, you might say you shouldn't pay for any **travel expenses** and yes, you would be within your rights to do so.

Here's a suggestion you could try that should make your current employee happy and not set a precedent that will come back to haunt you when it comes up again.

Set a dollar amount that you will pay round trip for a required trip to the headquarters' office. Make the amount enough to cover gas mileage and leave it there. That way you are not rewarding the employee for their decision to move away, but you also aren't penalizing them for needing to be in the office on a weekly basis.

This solution will work for a move that is within driving distance of the office. If more and more employees ask to live away from the office, you may want to develop a policy to cover these requests that would include:

- Prior approval must be granted before the move happens.
- If approved, specific details on reimbursement will be required.

- Negotiations to increase reimbursement must be held a minimum of three months in advance with no expectations they
will be granted.

Remember that any reimbursement arrangements made with one
employee must be granted to anyone, so take your time and think
this through before taking any action.

**Question: Some managers in my organization are questioning
whether employees need to use paid time off (PTO) as sick leave
since our working arrangements are now flexible. Is sick leave
becoming a thing of the past with so many employees working from
home (WFH)?**

Response: When traditional **sick leave** was the norm, the mental-
ity was to come to work anyway and power through. After the experiences of the pandemic of 2020 this attitude should have subsided,
but it seems it hasn't.

Employees have long felt pressure to work while sick, perhaps
because of heavy workloads that could get done only in the office. If
working arrangements are flexible and people are working asynchro-
nously, when and where the work gets accomplished becomes less
important. A worker with a bad cold may shut down on Thursday, for
example, and work on Saturday to make up the time.

However, should workers always be expected to make up time? If
you're ill, even with a seasonal cold, your body needs rest and time to
recover. A parent needs time off to care for a sick child. Medical and
dental appointments require time away during the workday.

Then there are situations involving medical procedures, for the
employee or family member, or sudden and serious medical events or
injuries, that require time and attention. Is an employee going to be
at a high level of productivity in any of these circumstances if there
is an expectation to power through or make up the time?

Sick leave, or the lack thereof, became a big issue during the pandemic. As a result, employees became acutely aware of their health

and welfare, and savvy employers who wanted to retain their talent took note. Benefit offerings in the area of health and welfare were expanded to address employees' needs.

To the managers questioning the need to use **paid time off** for health reasons: Is it that important to monitor how your employees are using their PTO? As long as the employees are either communicating their need for time off or advising they or a family member is ill and they need a day off, shouldn't that show they are responsible and accountable?

AVOIDING LEGAL PITFALLS

Question: Several employees have come to me requesting more flexible working arrangements. They would like to work from home exclusively, coming into the office only on rare occasions. They are willing to forego a salary increase in exchange for this arrangement. What are the pros and cons of allowing this practice?

Answer: Tread lightly with this issue. As appealing as it sounds to **forego a salary increase,** they may be thinking they are saving on commuting costs, lunches, and other costs associated with working in the office, as well as more flexibility to manage their home lives, but they will lose future benefits. For example:

- Assuming your organization offers a **retirement plan** such as a 401(k) that includes a match or employer contribution, a lower salary means less money is being contributed by both the employees (who contribute a percentage of their salary) and the employer. In the long term, this means less money in the account (contributions and growth over time) and a negative impact on retirement income.
- A lower salary can also negatively impact an employee's **Social Security benefit** at retirement.
- Future earnings can also be negatively impacted. Assume they forego an increase for two years. In year three, their base salary

and subsequent increase will be lower than it would have been if increases had not been withheld in the prior two years.

The risk for the organization is **pay inequity,** especially if this request is being made by women or **bipoc** (Black, Indigenous or other people of color) employees. You could be the target of a pay **discrimination** challenge if white men are receiving higher salaries than women or minorities (people in protected classes) for performing the same work. While there are a number of factors that can be considered to explain pay differences, a flexible work arrangement is not one of them.

Before discussing or making any adjustments to established pay practices, check with your legal advisors.

Question: More of our employees are working from home at least a few days each week. This makes it difficult to properly track everything. I've got several employees who are non-exempt, and I'm concerned about overtime. Without making it appear like we are spying, are time-tracking systems the way to go?

Answer: Remote and flexible work is filled with challenges when it comes to keeping track of hours for **non-exempt employees** who are, indeed, eligible for **overtime pay** under the Fair Labor Standards Act (FLSA) if they work beyond forty hours a week. Without proper documentation, if an employee claims they are due overtime, an employer will find it difficult to prove otherwise.

There is a fine line between keeping track of hours versus keeping track of employees' every move throughout the workday. Employers need to strike the right balance when employees are working remotely, while ensuring they are in compliance with wage and hour laws.

Time-tracking systems are effective in helping you meet this goal. Beyond these systems, it's important to have good processes in place, starting with communication. As a manager, this is where you play a key part.

- Let your nonexempt employees know the purpose of the system is to protect their rights. Advise them that they are entitled to receive overtime if they work over forty hours a week. Stress that the organization monitors their hours for this purpose.
- Inform employees that they need to have overtime approved in advance. While employers are still obligated to pay overtime, approved or not, it is wise to have an approval process in place to control costs. If an employee doesn't adhere to the process, nothing prohibits an employer from disciplining them.

Beyond this, you want to establish trust. Let employees know you value their privacy. Since many of these systems have surveillance capabilities, be upfront with employees if it is part of the system you use. If possible, turn these features off. Assure employees you will not be monitoring their every action. Finally, if employees have concerns about overtime or surveillance, listen to them and address their concerns. Talk to your organization's HR, legal, and technical advisors to get any answers you may need.

Question: I have an employee who has been calling in sick more than usual. I don't want to be asking too many personal questions or violating any laws, but I'm concerned about their health. Is there something I should be doing?

Answer: You have good instincts. There is sometimes a fine line between genuine concern and legal pitfalls, so your hesitation to question the employee is certainly understandable.

Employees can trigger the protections of the **Family Medical Leave Act (FMLA)** without referencing it when they ask for time off in relation to an illness, a surgery, or the birth of a child, for instance. The FMLA offers unpaid, job-protected leave to eligible employees who have serious health conditions, need to care for a family member with serious health conditions, or for the birth or adoption of a child.

It is also available to eligible employees in circumstances related to a family member's call to active duty or to care for a family member who became ill or injured while on active military duty. The FMLA allows employees to take this leave for a maximum of twelve weeks in a twelve-month period, and it covers public agencies, schools, and private employers with fifty or more employees.

It can be important for supervisors to understand the basics of the FMLA. Be aware that there are administrative requirements that can be extensive. For example, there are recordkeeping and notice requirements to which the employer must adhere. The employer has the right to receive notification and medical certification from the employee. While managers may not be responsible for administering the leave themselves, and need not know all the intricacies, they do need to know enough to understand when they need to elevate leave requests to HR, who can sort out all the details.

In this situation, it would be prudent to alert HR about the chronic absenteeism for illness, and let them initiate a conversation with the employee about the potential need for FMLA leave. If you get any push back from the employee, stress that you are concerned that they receive all the benefits to which they are entitled, but more importantly, for their health.

Question: I'm new to my current employer, and I just learned that we don't pay overtime to any employees. The president (and owner) takes the stance that all of our employees are professionals so that exempts them from overtime. He also thinks that since he gives time off to anyone who works long hours, it's okay. Is he correct?

Answer: No, he's not correct on several levels. First, let's define what it means to be exempt from the overtime requirements of the **Fair Labor Standards Act** or FLSA. There are several categories of jobs that are **exempt**—Executive, Administrative, Professional, Outside Sales, and Computer Employee. All categories have a salary test, and each category has its own duties test, meaning that the job's requirements or the work that is performed in the position must adhere to the duties described in each category. It's one thing to say your employees are all professional—and hopefully they conduct themselves professionally in the workplace—but that doesn't mean they pass the test for overtime exemption.

Private employers cannot use **compensatory time** off in lieu of paying overtime either. The law requires that if an employee's job is not exempt from the overtime requirements, they must be paid time and a half for any hours worked over forty hours in a workweek. Keep in mind, there are some states that have a daily overtime requirement, meaning overtime is due for hours worked over eight hours in a day.

Finally, employees cannot waive their right to be paid overtime if they are entitled to it. That would be illegal.

Your real dilemma is how to address this with your boss. Start by getting information about the FLSA from the Department of Labor's website—www.dol.gov. Once there, search for Agencies, Wage & Hour Division, Fair Labor Standards Act. You'll be able to find information about the salary test and the duties test for each category of exemption. You can present this information and make the business case for taking further corrective action, which should include contacting an employment attorney who can help you with some basic wage and hour compliance. Also let your boss know that if the **Department of Labor** audits your practices and finds they are not compliant, he'll be liable for back pay.

CLOSING THOUGHTS

Compensation and rewards are complicated issues, and this section gives you a great deal of information to help you navigate the murky waters of paying and rewarding employees. Keep in mind you want to pay fairly and competitively, and if you have a compensation philosophy, it will assist your decision making. Today's complicated work environment with hybrid and virtual work situations, and employees wanting to live where they want without regard to where the organization is physically located, is creating new challenges for managers. This section should point you in the right direction as you work to pay fairly.

SECTION 4

HELPING EMPLOYEES GROW AND DEVELOP

YOUR EMPLOYEES ARE on the move, or at least they should be. What could be more rewarding as a manager than to be part of seeing your great employees improve their skills so they can grow into new opportunities with your organization? That's what this section is all about—managers encouraging their employees to become life-long learners while they thrive in your dynamic culture. It's crucial to provide development opportunities that align with your organization's needs.

There are so many new ways to develop staff including gamification and microlearning. However, don't overlook traditional approaches such as mentoring, performance management, 360 evaluations, and the endless online opportunities. These topics and more are covered in this section.

Question: I keep hearing that it is a good business strategy to create a *learning culture* in our workplace. What is it, and how do we make it happen?

Answer: In a **learning culture**, all staff members are encouraged to be life-long learners by continuing to add to their knowledge and skill set, allowing them to perform at their highest possible level. Talk about a win-win proposition. The employee develops a new skill that can benefit your organization as well as their career growth. Building a learning culture potentially impacts productivity and can have a powerful impact on the employee experience. It's a wonder that every organization doesn't want a learning culture.

Creating a learning culture starts on the first day an employee joins your organization. Make part of your **onboarding process** a discussion about your plans for your new hires to learn and grow. Let them know how much you value learning and development, and share the opportunities you have for them to continue to add to their body of knowledge.

Consider having managers create **individual development plans** for each employee early in their time with you. This starts them off with the understanding that learning is valued and an integral part of your culture. Share your commitment to learning by recognizing employees who complete a program or get a certificate in a new subject. This is a way to make it obvious to everyone that learning is critical in your organization.

When you do in-house learning and development programs, build in a feedback mechanism so that you are constantly improving your offerings. Consider putting together a resource library to make it easy for your staff to access topics they are interested in.

Finally, one of the things that employees today want most, especially members of the younger generation, is the opportunity to grow and learn. Talk about a retention strategy.

There are so many ways you can bring skill building activities to your staff, so get started right away and create and nurture a learning culture.

Question: I've been managing a team for a year, and I'm getting to know my team members. I want to start developing them, but I don't know where to begin. What should I be looking at to determine each employee's development needs?

Answer: Congratulations for taking this step. **Career development** offers an opportunity for manager and employee to work collaboratively to enhance the employee's performance, prepare them for future assignments and responsibilities, and to contribute to the organization's goals. So it's important to consider the needs of both the employee and the organization.

When you look at the organization's needs, consider where your department is now and how it's function and contributions might change in the near future and over the next several years. Then consider if these changes will require your team to have new or different knowledge and skills.

Next, you'll want to assess each individual employee's skills, abilities, and potential for development. If you have a formal **performance evaluation** process, this is a good place to start, but don't forget your own observations of their performance and behavior.

Bring the employee into the process. Have meetings with them to discuss their interests and career goals along with any potential future opportunities. Make sure that their goals and interests align with those of the organization. Once you settle on a direction, encourage the employee to work with you to create an **individual development plan** or IDP. An IDP will typically include:

1. A clear statement of professional goals and objectives
2. Steps and activities to achieve them
3. Work opportunities or assignments of interest for the short and long term
4. An assessment of the necessary qualifications to perform those assignments
5. An assessment of training and development needed to prepare for those assignments

The final step in the IDP is to identify developmental activities along with some target dates for completion. Developmental activities can include:

- Education—certificate programs, conferences, seminars, and webinars
- Self-study—reading, podcasts, and blogs

- On-the-job training and cross training
- Participation in professional organizations
- Coaching
- Working with a mentor
- Virtual learning
- Participation in projects and on teams, task forces, or committees
- Stretch assignments

Clearly, creating an IDP must be a collaborative effort. You, as a manager and career coach, are likely to see things differently than the employee. You also have a broader view of the organization. This may seem like work, but your employees will become quickly engaged, and it will pay off.

Question: I encourage my team members to attend workshops and take training courses. How can I be sure what they are attending is relevant to their jobs and if they are applying what they learn?

Answer: Employee development is clearly a partnership between an employee and their manager. Your attitude is positive in wanting your employees to get the most out of their development. Surveys regularly show that professional development is a key driver of **employee satisfaction** and **retention**. These are two more reasons to do it right.

When your employees first sign up for a learning event, go over the objectives with them to make sure it will best meet their needs and the organization's needs. Consider if it will help the employee in their current job or prepare them for future assignments and opportunities. If they are going to be learning about new developments in their field, make sure the program is being delivered by a credible source.

Afterwards, review with the employee what they learned. This type of follow-up sends a powerful message and aligns the thinking between you and the employee. Things you can do include the following:

- If there is course material, go over it with them.
- Ask questions: What did they learn? Are there things they don't understand?
- Inquire if they think other team members would benefit from the same workshop or course.
- Give them assignments where they can apply and practice what they learned.
- Let the employee know if they are effectively applying what they learned to their assignments. If they are not, it's a great opportunity for coaching.

If the learning was about new or emerging developments, have the employee share what was learned with other team members and managers. This positions the employee to be the subject matter expert—the go-to person for what's new. What better way to **motivate** employees?

Having the employee take the lead on a new initiative also gives you, the manager, the opportunity to learn something from your employee. This is an excellent way to demonstrate your interest and partnership in the employee's learning.

Question: Our organization conducts a great deal of training, primarily for an external client base. I want to make sure any training we do, whether webinars or in-person training, is useful and effective since these sessions reflect on the entire organization. More importantly, I want my team to shine. Any guidance I can share with my staff so they are confident their audiences will be informed and impressed?

Answer: Kudos to you for taking the time to help your staff in these very visible assignments. Whether it's an online **webinar** or an in-person **presentation**, here are some tips:

- Include only relevant content. Edit out anything not originally built for the webinar's topic.

- A good rule of thumb is to limit the total time to one hour—forty-five minutes to present and fifteen minutes for Q&As from the audience. If you can't meet this guideline, then cut something out. Times may vary if presenting in other venues, such as conferences. Nevertheless, honor the time that's allotted.
- Have structure and don't wing it. Divide the program into blocks using the topics you plan to cover. You'll have some introductory material and some ending material, so plan approximately ten minutes for each block or segment, depending on the number of segments you have.
- Practice in advance. Review and rewrite bullets and talking points. This will keep you on track and succinct, ensuring that the audience remains engaged. If you do, they'll want to come back for more.
- If slides are being used, make sure they are engaging.
- Part of practice is timing the webinar. You want to make sure you can cover all of the useful information you plan to share with the audience in forty-five minutes or the allotted time.

If you are advertising or promoting webinars or in-person events to external audiences:

- Use an easy-to-understand description that tells people the title (make it informative—fifty to seventy characters maximum). Include what you'll cover (keep it brief—fifty words or less), who will present, and the length. Include registration instructions.
- Send registrants: one (1) email to confirm their registration, one (1) email to remind them, and one (1) email to announce a replay or recording afterward. Nothing is more annoying than getting multiple and constant emails before and after.

Follow these rules and your staff will wow their audiences, learn some things, and make future webinars and training even better. For less-experienced or new trainers, consider sending them to presentation skills training.

Question: We sometimes put our own training programs together, and I want to be sure we are focusing our outreach to adults. Can you provide some tips about how adults learn so we can make our programs successful?

Answer: Adults do learn differently, so your instincts are right. For starters, adults can't be forced to learn. By finding a way to let them see *what's in it for me,* your chance of successful learning increases. Here are other things to keep in mind when developing your **training programs** for **adult learners:**

- Adults need to feel as if the new information and/or skill you are presenting will make them more productive or more marketable. What is the payoff for them for their investment in time? Today's employees are anxious to add to their skill set and crave development. This means you should have a group of hungry people who are ready, willing, and able to learn something new. Don't let them down. If you do, you may not get a second chance to train them again.
- Adult learners need to be taught in very different ways. Take time before putting your program together to research the people in the group. Learn as much as possible about what they do and who they are. The more you know about them the better you can tailor your presentation to meet their needs.
- Adults respond to real-life and relevant examples and applications that are industry specific. If you are presenting to a small nonprofit organization, don't use examples from Fortune 100 companies or your audience will tune you out. Do your research so that you are credible to your audience.
- Adults like to practice what they are learning, so build in simulations and exercises for your participants. However, know your audience before asking participants to stand up in front

of others and try something new. Some people will jump right in and be part of the program while others will shut down. Another reason why your preparation and knowledge of your audience is a key to success.

- Adult learners like to share what they already know about a topic. Build in time for people to share stories and examples, but don't let their past experiences dominate the session. Letting people talk for a while and using some of what they share in your training session helps to build on what they already know.

Question: We are considering starting a mentoring program but are not sure what steps to take. Can you point us in the right direction?

Answer: Mentoring is a win-win development strategy for your organization and your staff members. It is a no- or low-cost process that not only can provide development opportunities for your team members, it can also be valuable in the hiring process. Many job applicants want to know if your organization provides mentors to new hires. If you do, it may give you an edge in hiring the best talent available.

A broad definition of a mentor is anyone who has knowledge or experience the other person doesn't have. Mentors don't have to be senior managers or long-time employees. In fact, many organizations are now doing "reverse mentoring" and having their millennials helping older staff members master our ever-changing technology.

When you are putting a **mentoring program** together—whether it is formal or informal—consider these things:

- Be sure the goals of the program link to your organization's goals or to a specific development plan and you have leadership support.
- Include clear definitions, guidelines, and structure in the program. Do not make it too complicated, but have goals and deliverables that allow you to measure success.
- Have a start and end time—maybe a six-month schedule with opportunities to extend or contract as needed.

- Provide training for mentors as well as resources for them to use as they work with their mentee.
- Have an evaluation process, and be prepared to modify the program as needed.

Mentoring can easily be done remotely, so don't stop your program if your organization is virtual or hybrid. Your employees will thank you if you provide mentoring.

Question: You mentioned something called reverse mentoring in the last question. Can you explain more about how it works and how we could use it?

Answer: Traditional **mentoring programs** usually pair a long-term employee with a new hire or a seasoned staff member with a younger person. **Reverse mentoring** is a partnership between a junior-level person and a senior-level staff member in which the junior-level staffer shares their expertise.

The most frequent use of reverse mentoring is when there is a gap in the digital skills of a more senior employee. Pairing two people with different skill sets and empowering the junior staff member to share their knowledge can be a very powerful experience for both people.

Reverse mentoring programs can do more than transfer skills from one to the other. They can help facilitate respectful relationships between members of different generations in your workplace. When people get to know each other as human beings and not just work colleagues, productivity increases are likely to result.

Participating in a reverse mentoring program could potentially help you retain a talented and highly marketable employee.

Here are some things to consider if you decide reverse mentoring might be beneficial:

- Do some research before announcing a program. Talk to some employees and gauge the interest level.
- Carefully match the participants by skill levels and their interest in participating. As with any new program, your first try

will set the stage for future success, so be extra careful on your first batch of participants. Consider doing a pilot before rolling out your program. Be sure you have the full commitment of the senior staff member since they need to fully participate for the program to be a success.

- Use your successes to market the program to others.
- Set goals and program guidelines before getting started. Make sure each participant is clear on the parameters. Review and revise the goals as the program progresses.
- Train the mentors to be successful. They may need help about how to structure a session or other advice. Give them a safe place to go with questions or challenges they face.
- Do frequent check ins and make changes as needed.

Give this a try. Not only can it be a successful retention tool, it's a great development opportunity for the junior staff member as well.

Question: There are many HR programs in place in our organization, but I'm not sure about my role as a manager in most of them. I'm particularly interested in my role in the performance evaluation program. Can you give me some insights?

Answer: A common misconception arises when organizations debate who's responsible for overseeing employee performance and what it entails. You mention the **performance evaluation program** in your organization, referring to it as an HR program. In that it deals with employees or people, then it could be considered an HR program—but not a program that HR owns.

Let's look at this from a broader perspective, namely **performance management** and a systems approach toward it. The purpose of performance management systems is to ensure that employees, individually and collectively, are producing their best products or services. Managing the individual performance of each individual employee is clearly one of the most important responsibilities of any manager.

Performance management is a process that should start on an employee's first day, and managers can set the framework for success by providing a copy of the employee's job description. They should have a discussion with the employee about their job duties, the manager's and the organization's expectations for the position, and expectations about job-related behaviors. It's also a good time to discuss goals and objectives, at least for the short term. Finally, brief employees about the organization's culture and value and what success looks like.

Performance management is something that should be ongoing and not an annual event. Returning to your mention of the performance evaluation program, it is often a part of the performance management system that HR often designs and oversees. It's a way to document employee performance, but it should not be the *only* way.

Managers should be continually evaluating each employee's performance against the job's requirements and standards for success. This includes noting (and documenting) all incidents (positive and negative) throughout the year, and having frequent conversations with the employees. This approach not only ensures that performance management is a process, it also guards against any surprises occurring when a formal evaluation meeting takes place.

Question: You just provided some good insights about performance management and my role as a manager. When I spoke with HR, they told me the same thing and emphasized the need for frequent feedback. Could you provide some practical guidance about having frequent conversations with employees about their performance?

Answer: Frequent, on-going **feedback** lets employees know how they are doing, that they are making contributions, and that they are valued by the organization. It is a powerful way to motivate and retain staff.

Provide feedback as soon as you notice something noteworthy—positive, not just corrective, in nature. Let the employee know what you've observed—positive or corrective. Use specific examples, not vague statements like, "You're doing a great job." Be sure to tell the employee what expectations are and are not being met.

Go on to explain the impact of what you observed. For example, "When you delivered the report early, it gave others on the team additional time to complete their portions of the project." This gives the employee the opportunity to understand why the impact was great or why it was problematic. It allows you both the chance to explore either potential problems or better outcomes.

From there, you can talk about what should be continued and what needs to change. Using this approach, you're letting the employee know:

- What is working and what's not; and
- What they can do to be more effective.

Unless immediate action is called for, for example you witness a safety issue that needs correction, be sure to set aside time for these meetings—even if you only need a few minutes.

- Create a positive and communicative atmosphere.
- Take the time to listen and ask questions. You should be engaging in a dialogue with the employee.
- Ask what, if anything, you can do to assist the employee going forward.
- Finally, this may be a chance to explore potential, future opportunities for the employee.

Question: I want to work with my team to set goals for the year so that we all are on the same page. I also want to set goals so I can hold them accountable for the work they are tasked with doing. How can I make goal setting part of how we work together?

Answer: You raise a good point: How can you hold people accountable if they don't know what they are working to achieve? Well, the best way is to start at the beginning of the year or the start of a project, setting goals together so that everyone is on the same page. Employees tend to achieve more if they have a part in **goal setting** rather than having goals set by their manager or someone else.

You've probably heard about a formula for goal setting using the SMART acronym. Here's how the formula works with a twist:

S SPECIFIC. A goal needs to be well defined and focused. Think about the who, what, and why to help you be as specific and focused as possible.

M MEASURABLE. What gets measured gets done, so how will you determine success? What measures do you need either short-term or long-term to measure success?

A ACHIEVABLE. Nothing is more demotivating than having a goal that is out of reach. Be sure that the goal can be met, but it's okay if it's a bit of a stretch. You want it to be a challenge but not impossible.

R RELEVANT. A goal should be linked to your organization's or your team's current work or project.

T TIMEBOUND. A goal should have a date or time attached to it to ensure completion.

As a manager, your role is to work to set the goals and build in milestones where you check in with the employee to see how they are doing. If they are having issues, you'll want to help them find solutions. This is not a place or time for you to micromanage. Rather, it is a time for you to be supportive. Do they need resources? Do they need more time? Does the goal need to be revised? Give your employees frequent feedback as they work toward goal achievement.

You can use the goals and the achievement of those goals as one basis for your performance reviews. However you use the goal-setting process, keep it alive, and talk about it frequently. It will help you keep your staff accountable and your organization productive.

Question: One of our managers suggested we do 360 reviews for some functions or maybe even all of our employees. Is this a good idea and if so, how do they work?

Answer: These are formally called **multi-rater reviews**. You gather a group of people who have some connection to the employee you want rated and ask them a series of questions relating to that employee's performance. They can provide you with good information, but only if you take care to select the right people to do the rating and those people are carefully trained in the process.

It is a time-consuming process, and in order to maintain confidentiality, many organizations use consultants to prepare the survey, analyze the results, and convey them to the employee. This can be costly to the organization. Therefore, if you decide to go this route, you may want to target specific departments or positions where the information would be particularly impactful and useful.

A **360 review** is just that—a full circle view of the employee or the function. For example, if you were reviewing a department manager you'd want to include:

- Their direct supervisor
- Several peers
- Several subordinates
- People outside the organization such as customers, suppliers, etc.

There may be times when an organization's leadership is asked to participate, but that is rare.

If you are using a consultant, they will work with you to prepare the questions and structure the survey in a way that the employee doesn't know who said what. If you are doing this on your own, you will create the questions and prepare the raters before they start the process. You will get the data and then present it to the employee being rated.

Another way to do 360 reviews is to personally interview raters using the same questions. There is some value to this as you can ask follow-up questions, but the downside is the amount of time it requires. Again, using a consultant can be helpful here especially when the results are shared with the employee.

As with any evaluation process, the key is what you do with the information collected. So, consider how you will follow up with any issues that are uncovered. These could include coaching, counseling, or mentoring if development is warranted.

Bottom line, this is not a simple process and is extremely time intensive. However, it certainly has its benefits if done correctly.

Question: Any advice on how to handle this situation: The parent of one of my employees called me to discuss my recent performance review of their child—a twenty-something, college-educated professional. I was so stunned that I'm not sure I said the right thing. The employee is mortified, but I don't want to take it out on them.

Answer: We feel your pain and admit that we're not surprised that this happened to you. The issue of **helicopter parents** seems to be with us to stay.

Hopefully, this will never happen to you again, but if it does, here are some suggestions as to what you can do to be professional in any interaction with family members:

- Stay calm.
- Stay focused on what is said so you can respond appropriately.
- Take notes to help you stay focused.
- Let the person tell you their issue before you respond.
- If conversation turns accusatory, cut it off.

After the parent has run out of steam (hopefully before your desire for revenge kicks in), try this. In as calm a voice as you can, remind the parent that it is totally inappropriate for you to be speaking with them about their offspring. The only person with whom you will discuss your team member's performance is the employee themselves. Thank the parent for the call and do your best to end it there.

If that doesn't work, repeat what you just said until such time as the parent gets the message and you can end the call.

If there is a concrete point the parent makes such as *my child has never received any grade below an A and you gave a B*, you can share that the rating system your organization uses is not equivalent to a grading system in education. You might share the words that support your rating system and how it is used in your organization. Only you will be able to determine if sharing any specifics about the rating system will be helpful.

One final suggestion if you aren't getting through to the parent is to ask them politely if the employee—in this case, their child—knows they are calling. This sometimes shames them into ending their rant.

It is up to you as to whether to tell the employee about the call, but no matter what, if you keep your cool and give the person a chance to vent, it usually ends right here. We wish you well.

Question: I'd like to improve my coaching abilities but struggle with how to move the conversation forward. Do you have any ideas for me on the questions I should be asking to get the results I know coaching can produce?

Answer: You're right. **Coaches** use questions as one of their tools when working with people to find answers to help the person being coached, or the coachee, navigate the issues they are facing. Many people are not naturally reflective and struggle with the deep thinking needed to move beyond where they are.

There are no right or wrong questions or answers. Questions should be carefully selected to fit the situation the person you are **coaching** is in. Here are some possible questions to consider:

1. What would or could you gain or lose from moving in this direction?
2. What else could you do to resolve the situation?
3. How will you know you've succeeded?
4. Why do you think this might have happened?
5. What might be another way to resolve or respond to this issue?
6. What have you tried so far to change/resolve this situation?
7. What are the underlying issues?
8. What emotions are you experiencing?

9. How is this affecting your family?
10. What are you afraid of?
11. What if money wasn't an issue?
12. What, if anything, gives you energy around this issue?
13. What's your gut telling you?
14. What don't you want to lose?
15. What would achieving this do for you? For your job? For your family?
16. What's the end result you are looking for?
17. How could you make a change and reduce the risk involved?
18. What would success look like?
19. Which of your values does this impact?
20. Bottom line, what would you like to see differently?

One way of asking coaching questions is to ask the same question but from a different angle or perspective. Your goal as a coach is to get your coachee to think differently about a challenge or problem they're facing. The coach doesn't solve problems. Rather, the coach helps the coachee to see a path forward and helps them have the courage to take it.

While we admire your willingness to coach your employees, there may be times when it is more productive to bring in a **certified coach** who has extensive training and experience in a variety of coaching situations. When needed, ask your professional network for recommendations.

NAVIGATING THE CHANGING WORKPLACE

Question: Changing technologies and new ways of working are part of the workplace, the way jobs are performed, and the skills employees need to do their jobs. As a manager, I'm concerned that I'm not doing enough to help my team keep their skills current. At the same time, I don't want to overburden them. How do we keep up?

Answer: Your observation is correct. Add to it the pressure to find employees with the new skills, and employers and managers have increased challenges. They not only have to plan for current and future staffing needs, they have to examine changing skills needed for current jobs and future jobs.

Hopefully, to meet changing skills requirements, your organization has seen the value of investing in their existing employees. By that we mean, developing their employees and equipping them with the skills they need to be successful, referred to as **reskilling**—learning new skills for a different job and **upskilling**—learning new skills needed in existing positions.

Organizations are engaging in creative ways to meet the objective of maintaining an effective workforce. Consider the following examples, some of which can be incorporated with **on-the-job training**:

- Sponsoring **job-sharing programs** so employees can learn new roles
- Implementing **mentorship programs**, especially ones focused on having younger employees teach technology skills to more seasoned colleagues
- Creating in-house apprentice programs
- Offering in-house courses, especially technology courses, taught by current staff

Beyond what's offered internally, there are other resources that organizations can explore.

- Look at community colleges. They offer a wide variety of skills-based courses.
- Many communities offer public workshops and seminars taught by professionals in the particular field.

Your organization can take advantage of the many virtual learning platforms and sources, such as podcasts, webinars, and YouTube videos. Don't overlook emerging trends such as gamification and microlearning. They are delivered on mobile friendly platforms that are easy to access and increase participation.

The challenge to attract and retain good employees is nothing new. However, employees are rethinking their options in new ways. One thing they crave is development opportunities, so make them available. You may need to be creative to accelerate new skills development, but doing so will support your retention strategy.

Question: I was recently speaking with colleagues in my industry. One of them referenced something called gamification, and he said that his company was using it for employee development. What exactly is gamification?

Answer: With work and workers becoming more mobile, expect to see greater reliance on technology such as gamification apps. **Gamification** infuses game-like elements into skill development and other areas of learning. If properly developed, games are engaging and encourage employees to complete tasks and meet their goals resulting in improved productivity.

Organizations are using gamification to focus learning on targeted objectives for individual employees. It works because it makes the learning process fun while doing something they would have to do anyway.

Gamification has been used in employee recognition programs where contests are created and points are accrued that can be used for tangible prizes. Organizations have used gamification apps for on-the-job training for new hires. It's also a great tool to support onboarding, team building, and product and sales training.

Mobile apps make the information accessible and provide employees the ability to learn and earn recognition anywhere and at any convenient time, making it well suited for a mobile or remote workforce. It's also appealing to younger workers, making it a great retention tool.

Simple uses of gamification include digital checklists of tasks where employees can track their progress, or actionable goals to complete before new responsibilities are assigned. These game-like features motivate employees to accomplish their objectives. It also makes repetitive tasks more interesting and can generate continuous feedback on employee performance, another attractive feature for younger workers.

Explore the options that are constantly evolving. In your browser, look for gamification in the workplace or for employee development. You'll find organizations offering ready-made solutions and others that offer solutions customized to your needs. You are sure to find ones that meet your needs.

Question: Something I've heard about recently is microlearning, a type of learning that is used for employee development. It sounds like it's an abbreviated form of learning that might not deliver sufficient information on a given topic. How effective is it?

Answer: Microlearning is turning content and learning into little bits and pieces. It's a way of delivering learning. Think of it as small learning units and short-term learning activities.

Delivered on mobile platforms and devices, usually in three- to ten-minute bursts, it offers learning that employees can access when and where they need it. Information is usually developed in bit-sized pieces or short bursts of focused, right-sized content typically shared one at a time or for a specific purpose. For example, microlearning can present real-time and life-like scenarios that help employees relate to the particular topic. Learning modules delivered in traditional methods can later be augmented into bits that reinforce the classroom learning.

In the area of skills development, an individual task can be presented in a module. With mobile technology, employees can rewatch each module to enhance their learning and knowledge retention. Once they are comfortable and have mastered the first task, they can move on to the next module and apply and build on their knowledge.

There are a number of reasons why microlearning is effective.

- Employees can learn at their own pace and convenience.
- Content is focused on relevant, specific information, making retention easier.
- Modules are smaller with less information, making comprehension easier.
- Modules match our attention spans, which are shorter than you may think. Our brains aren't wired to focus for hours on end on one thing (learning or performing a task).
- As information changes, it's easy to update the short modules.

Microlearning is a way to get employees involved in their own learning. Its very nature empowers employees with the message that they are in charge of, and play an active role in, their own development. Given the opportunity to learn a new skill, for example, then put it to use immediately while the information is fresh in their minds, will position them to want more.

Question: I'm hearing a lot about how our new reality at work is emphasizing the importance of "soft skills." I'm not even sure what this means but certainly need some help with why soft skills are even more important now than ever. Can you point me in the right direction?

Answer: Interesting that **soft skills** are getting attention. The past few years, we've all been focused on how to maximize technology, but now we're realizing that soft skills are equally or maybe even more important for success.

Hard skills are skills which are quantifiable, measurable, or doable. A hard skill can be a technical skill such as knowing how to do a particular task. As an example, knowing how to use Microsoft Excel would be a hard skill—either you know it or you don't.

On the other hand, soft skills aren't about having the ability to do something or perform a task or service. They aren't easy to quantify and frequently involve interpersonal skills. An example of a soft skill is the ability to delegate work to others or to motivate a team.

One of the most important soft skills is the ability to communicate. There is almost no job in our world where communication isn't necessary. Managers need to be able to clearly issue directions or share goals with their employees. Staff members need to be able to share their progress or ask for clarification from a manager or mentor. Managers and staff members need to be able to resolve any conflict or issue that gets in the way of their working together. Working in a hybrid environment has put greater emphasis on the ability to communicate.

There are other important soft skills that are keys to success at work including:

- Flexibility
- Teamwork
- Humility
- Empathy
- Conflict resolution
- Time management

If you are not already offering training on soft skills, you should seriously consider doing so. Any of them can be developed with practice and experience. Check out YouTube for videos where you can practice a soft skill. It will be well worth your time to do this for yourself; but as a manager, don't overlook helping your staff upgrade their soft skills as well. Your employees will thank you for investing time and resources into their development.

Question: I am a firm believer in the value and the impact of coaching my employees. But now that I am managing a hybrid workforce, I'm struggling and not sure if I am being effective. Are there some things I should do differently when coaching my remote staff?

Answer: Thank you for asking about this very important part of management these days. **Coaching** finally has been recognized as a powerful development tool, so it is more important than ever that managers make coaching a high priority.

However, there are challenges in our hybrid or totally remote environment. Let's examine some of them:

- How to establish and build the trust necessary to coach
- How to hold the powerful conversations needed in coaching
- How to challenge assumptions and get employees to move from intentions to action

Coaching requires a lot of faith in the other person. And one of the qualities of a great coach is someone who sees potential in the person to be coached, or the coachee. Great coaches believe that people are naturally talented, resourceful, make good decisions, and solve their own problems with just a little bit of guidance. This is how you build trust that makes coaching so powerful.

Here's the big news—none of what a coach does depends on geography. Coaching also requires a high level of accountability, and great coaches model accountability for themselves and others. We're not talking about the kind of accountability that depends on physical presence or where someone sits in the organization. It is about a sense of personal power and self-respect that can be shared from anyplace.

Most successful coaches find phone coaching to be highly effective, and they felt this way long before we were in a pandemic. Many coaching conversations take place on the phone. It's amazing how much better we listen to each other on the phone than when we are sitting across the table from each other.

Coaches don't make people take action. They ask good questions that get the coachee thinking in a different way. They challenge assumptions by suggestion—not demands. There is a list of questions earlier in this section that you can review.

Remember, where you are physically should not impact your ability to be a good coach. Phone coaching is highly effective, so give it a try. It's very likely you will find your coaching has the desired outcome.

AVOIDING LEGAL PITFALLS

Question: We are planning an offsite meeting. The facilitator for a team-building exercise wants us to distribute a questionnaire in advance. One question references the employee's year of birth. I'm uneasy with the question. Am I overreacting?

Answer: Actually, this is an excellent catch. Asking about year of birth could result in a claim of **age discrimination**.

A good rule to guide you: If you wouldn't ask a question on a job application or in an interview, then don't ask it during employment unless there is a business need to know. For this particular question, the exception or business need would be for benefit purposes such as life and health insurance, just as you'd ask an employee—not an applicant—about dependents for the specific purpose of benefits coverage.

Have you asked the facilitator why they want this information? If not, do so. Perhaps they want to break the group into smaller teams with multigenerational representation for a particular exercise. If that's the case, it's something you can help with since you know your employees and should have an idea of the broad generational category each one might fit into.

I'd also ask the facilitator for more information about the types of exercises the employees will be engaging in. Do they want a cross section of other diversity dimensions (gender, race, organizational function, for example) on each of the teams? This would be an excellent idea since all of our dimensions of diversity influence how we look at situations and solve problems.

Consider varying the composition of the teams for different exercises. Having the generational mix may be good if the focus of the exercise is mentoring, for example. If the exercise is to look at how years of experience or tenure with the organization affects people's approach, then look at those factors. Mixing up the teams' composition also gives employees the opportunity to work with and get to know a number of different colleagues.

Work with the facilitator in advance to get the best results, and good luck with your meeting.

Question: It is certainly difficult managing my team's performance when I don't see them every day. In addition, I've heard there can be legal risks. Can you explain this and give me some tips on effectively managing remote teams?

Answer: Managers will have to manage differently when staff isn't in the office every day, especially when some are and some are not. Tension can develop between employees who work in the office and those who work from home or remotely. When conversations happen organically among staff members who are in the office, crucial information might be shared. If remote employees are not given the same information, they will not only feel alienated, they may also be missing out on potential opportunities.

As a manager, you need to be sure to pass the information along to remote employees as quickly as possible, so they are not disadvantaged. Otherwise, there might be the reality or perception that critical information has been withheld, a problem if a larger percentage of remote employees are members of protected classes.

Managers also have to be diligent about not giving, or creating the perception of giving, **preferential treatment** to workers in the office, such as giving them better assignments. Legal risks can result, for example, if more remote workers are women and more in-office workers are men and the men are getting more visible assignments and **development opportunities.**

When staff is not in the office every day, managers must be proactive by staying in touch and checking in with staff working remotely to understand how they are doing and how their work is progressing.

Some things to keep in mind about **performance management** of remote workers:

- Maintain awareness of remote work performance and monitor how employees are doing in both their roles and their careers. Practice real-time feedback. It gives employees a better understanding of how they are doing on a frequent basis.
- Conduct frequent, one-on-one meetings. They help managers understand employee's needs and issues.
- Keep a pulse on remote teams. Track collaboration, productivity, and results. More importantly, get feedback on the team's challenges and struggles either through simple surveys or individual conversations.
- When assessing performance, maintain a focus on outcomes.
- As always, document the conversations you have with your team.

All of these steps are important parts of managing your team's performance. You'll get the best from your team and create a positive work environment.

CLOSING THOUGHTS

Today's employees have made it loud and clear that they stay with organizations that help them enhance their skill sets. They are passionate about learning and personal development, and if your organization doesn't provide what they want, they will find a place that does. So, providing development opportunities isn't a *nice thing to do* anymore, it is an absolute requirement for success. Don't miss out on the joy of watching your team members improve their skills.

SECTION 5

UNDERSTANDING POLICIES AND PRACTICES

POLICIES, PRACTICES, PROCEDURES, oh my. They are often misunderstood and interpreted as a way of constraining managers. Quite the contrary. Policies are not intended to be, and should not be treated as, mandates. Rather, they should be guidance for managers when they have to deal with people issues—issues they expect as well as issues that are unexpected.

Well-written policies are developed with the managers and employees in mind, allowing for flexibility to address each unique situation. They help ensure consistency in addressing people issues. However, consistency doesn't mean rigidity. An employee with a good record who has worked for the organization for years will be given different consideration than a fairly new worker. Keep that in mind as a manager and use judgment when making decisions about people. For this reason, we cover more than just formal policies, but also practices reflecting how to treat people fairly and with respect.

Question: I've worked in organizations of different sizes and have noticed their approaches to policies appear to be just as varied—from little or no written policies and managers fending for themselves to more structured policies with guidance for managers and allowances for exceptions. **What are the purposes of policies, and is there a risk if they aren't enforced or exceptions are allowed?**

Answer: Different organizations take different approaches toward their policies. All things being equal, policies should be a foundation and reflection of an organization's **culture**—a guide to how things are done.

Human resource policies should be just that, guidance and not mandates. The reason is the situations you are dealing with involve **employee behavior,** which is not universal nor predictable in nature. Contrast that with a policy on expense reporting which is very straightforward regarding allowable versus unallowable expenses.

When managers and HR leaders are considering actions to take against policy violations, they must consider a number of things in addition to the violation itself. They are likely to look at the employee's employment history and tenure with the organization, the severity and the impact of the violation, and how other situations and similarly situated individuals were handled. In other words, they use judgment, which is an imperative. Exceptions to policies often occur when these other factors are considered.

There are some HR policies that exist in response to legal or regulatory guidelines, such as harassment policies. **The Equal Employment Opportunity Commission** issued guidance regarding the contents of an effective anti-harassment policy and complaint procedure. Many organizations tailor their policies on such guidance and would rarely make exceptions.

Policies do vary among organizations because of the nature of the industry. Manufacturing companies, for example, may have more stringent rules and policies around safety measures for good reason.

Smaller organizations may not see the need for extensive policies, but a total lack of policies could work to their disadvantage. Absent written policies, precedent will become your de facto policy, at least from a legal standpoint. The same holds true for policies that exist, but are not enforced nor followed consistently. In a challenge, the enforcement agencies or the courts will look to how similar situations were handled in the past.

Question: I recently obtained a graduate degree in management and just accepted my first management job with a new organization. How do I learn more about the organization's policies and practices, especially when it comes to people management?

Answer: Congratulations on your degree and your new position. You are off to a great start as a new manager by recognizing the importance of **HR policies** and people management issues.

Your first step should be to talk with your immediate manager to determine where you can find out more about the organization's policies. The **employee handbook** is likely the first place you'll look, but many organizations have more extensive management policy manuals depending on their size and complexity.

Take the time to get acquainted with the resources available, and that means reading the policies. You want to know the types of issues that are covered in the policies. Don't try to digest all of the information at once. It could be a daunting task, especially if you are in a large organization.

Inquire if there are any online training programs about the policies. Some organizations offer such training, tailored specifically to their policies, as a resource for new managers.

If your organization has an HR department or resource, schedule some time with them. Let them know you're interested in learning more about the policies. Have a meeting to discuss some of the more important policies, which can include **employee conduct, performance management, nondiscrimination** and equal employment opportunity (EEO), **anti-harassment,** and employee **leaves of absence.** Certainly, there may be more you would like to explore, but these will be a good starting place.

You can keep the conversation going. Creating a rapport with HR early in your management career will build a great deal of credibility for you. HR and your manager would much rather answer hypothetical questions now, rather than wait until being faced with a significant issue down the road.

Question: I'm reviewing my organization's Human Resource policies. Many of them are not much different from other places where I've worked, but I've often wondered about the difference between a performance management policy and a conduct policy. When does each apply?

Answer: You're not alone in being curious about the distinction. Many managers are.

Performance management focuses on how well employees are doing their job and whether they are meeting expectations set by management and/or industry standards. A performance management policy generally includes a process for managers to define performance expectations, provide continuous feedback to employees, and often to formally review performance at agreed to times. This process should include a goal setting and frequent informal check-ins to help the employee stay on track. Also, if performance falls below expectations or standards, a process for what happens next is included.

What happens next is often referred to as a **performance improvement plan** or PIP. It details tasks to be completed, dates for their accomplishment, and next steps if necessary.

Employee conduct, on the other hand, focuses on **workplace behavior.** The policy establishes and defines the standards of conduct that are not acceptable. It generally states that the list of behaviors described is not all-inclusive and that there can be other infractions that may result in **disciplinary action.**

A **progressive discipline** process is used to address conduct that is unacceptable. This may include counseling, verbal warnings, written warnings, suspensions, or termination. A fair and defensible progressive or corrective discipline process allows management flexibility in determining whether all steps should be used and when to use them.

So, when an employee's **performance** doesn't meet expectations, performance improvement plans are used to address deficiencies. If an employee is misbehaving—their **conduct** is disruptive—corrective or progressive discipline processes are implemented. If the employee is simultaneously having both performance and conduct problems, both processes can be used. If that's the case, be sure you check with your HR and legal advisers before taking action.

Question: My organization has a very comprehensive employee conduct policy that clearly defines types of conduct that is unacceptable. Is there really a need to have additional policies that address specific behavior, such as harassment or drug use?

Answer: It may sound like overkill, but for certain categories of behavior it may be necessary to have stand-alone policies. Sometimes it is driven by regulation or industry standards, or the size and nature of the organization may be the reason. These policies should work with broader conduct policies, especially when it comes to **progressive discipline**. Let's look at some common policies and what they include.

   Workplace Harassment. To address the effects of **sexual harassment**, the Equal Employment Opportunity Commission (EEOC) provides standards for a policy that addresses the issue and the employer's commitment to having a workplace free of all forms of harassment, not just sexual harassment. The policy should include a definition of harassment with clear explanations of prohibited conduct and define the responsibility of all employees, managers, and human resources to uphold the policy. Also included are an assurance against retaliation, a complaint process and investigation process with assurances of confidentiality to the extent possible, and a corrective action process when harassment has occurred.
   Drug Abuse. Organizations want to keep illicit drugs and impaired employees out of the workplace. Certain industries, such as transportation or nuclear energy, require drug tests, usually for safety purposes. Policies should prohibit employees from possessing,

using, manufacturing, purchasing, dispensing, or selling illegal drugs on the premises. There should be consequences for violation and provisions for referrals to the **Employee Assistance Program (EAP)** for drug, alcohol, and related mental health problems.

Workplace Violence. This type of behavior can be devastating, and organizations want more specific guidelines. A policy should clearly state that violence or threats of violence, including bullying, are not tolerated; define the prohibited conduct and provide examples; have disciplinary procedures for employees who engage in such behavior; include a reporting and investigation process; and have provisions for EAP referrals.

Electronic Media. In order to protect organization assets and provide security, organizations implement electronic media policies that define what is considered an unacceptable use of technology, and emphasize that any equipment and systems used are the property of the organization. These policies set expectations for the responsible use of technology, including the systems that support technology in the workplace such as email, internet access, and the organization's networks.

Question: The last two answers about HR policies were very helpful. Are there any other specific policies that are common for an organization to have?

Answer: There are certain policies that organizations generally consider implementing. They are:

Employment at Will. Since most organizations are at-will employers, you need either a formal policy or a statement that explains this relationship. At-will employment means that at any time, with or without notice, employees are free to join or leave their employer, and the organization is free to establish or terminate the employment relationship.

Equal Employment Opportunity (EEO). At the heart of an organization's desire to establish and maintain a fair, respectful, and inclusive workplace, they have a formal EEO policy or statement. At a minimum, it states that the organization prohibits discrimination based on all of the protections in the federal nondiscrimination laws—race, color, religion, national origin, and sex including sexual orientation and gender identity—as well as any additional protections under state or federal law.

Leaves of Absence. There are certain types of mandatory leave that include family and medical leave (FMLA) for eligible employers and employees, military leave, and leave for jury and witness duty. Employers may also provide bereavement leave, emergency leave including inclement weather, and other types of special leaves. Depending on the size of the organization and the nature and complexity of the leave requirements, some of these policies can be stand-alone while others can be bundled into one. Whatever the case, it is important for the policy to state who is eligible for the leave and whether it is paid or unpaid,

Layoff and Termination. The circumstances around how the employment relationship ends are varied and may be complex depending on the size and nature of the organization. Termination policies often provide guidance for both voluntary and involuntary terminations—including circumstances when these actions may be taken and the appropriate actions and approvals needed. Layoff policies address reductions in force, any associated legal requirements, and whether or not **severance pay** is provided.

Question: We're a small start-up and are curious about some of the basics of HR. We're wondering if we need an employee handbook, and, if so, where do we start and what should it contain?

Answer: Think of it this way—when you play a new game, don't you start by reading the rules? **Employee handbooks** are a very efficient and very practical way to communicate policies to your staff and to your managers. Your managers will appreciate having a place they can go to find out how your organization deals with issues so that they can respond to staff questions.

Employee handbooks typically contain policies and procedures, along with information about your vision, mission, values, and your organization's history. Including a welcome from the top leader in your organization, such as the CEO or executive director, sets the tone for how your organization views the relationship with your employees.

Don't use a generic handbook or borrow one from a previous employer. A handbook must be relevant to your organization. Consider engaging the services of an HR consultant to draft your handbook to be sure you cover all that needs to be included, followed by a review from an employment attorney.

There are some important things to consider as your handbook is crafted:

- Don't include too much detail on procedures. Your handbook is not an instruction manual on how to do the job. Consider creating a "Manager's Manual" as you grow.
- Do include an **employment at-will** disclaimer, and make sure no other statements contradict it.
- Do include a statement advising that you reserve the right to change or modify any policy and that you will notify employees if and when that happens.
- Do include an Acknowledgement Form even if the handbook is available only in soft copy. It's important that employees are held accountable for reading and understanding the handbook (and acknowledge they've received a copy). Repeat the acknowledgement process when new policies are added or when significant changes are made to existing policies.
- Do keep it friendly and conversational in tone (You're eligible for . . . versus The employee is eligible for . . .) and avoid jargon and acronyms.

- Do pay careful attention to be sure there are no inconsistencies in the completed document. Even if you engage outside assistance, the handbook is the organization's responsibility.

Review your handbook at least yearly followed by a briefing for all staff. It's to your advantage to take time to remind your staff of what's changed and what's in your handbook.

Question: Human Resources always stresses the importance of writing up employees whenever there is a problem. I feel like this approach is forcing managers to build a case for terminating an employee. What if the employee's performance or attitude improves? Am I missing something?

Answer: Don't ever underestimate the importance of maintaining and keeping **documentation**, which is what HR wants you to do. Documentation provides a record of what has occurred, so managers don't have to rely on their memory when they want to take action regarding an employee. These records support a number of management actions, including pay increases, promotions, recognition, job assignments, and yes, termination or other adverse actions.

Looking at positive situations, if you have an employee whose performance is always exceeding the expectations of the job, you will want to note specific examples, such as when tasks are accomplished ahead of deadlines, or when specific problems are anticipated and addressed. Your notes and examples can form the basis for justifying why you might select this employee for an assignment or promotion rather than others.

On the negative side, you may have an employee who begins to arrive late (for work or for meetings). If you overlook or fail to note these instances, they may be difficult to recall if a pattern of the behavior begins to emerge. If you keep notes, you will be in a better position no matter what occurs. Should the pattern correct itself, or the employee improves as you suggested, then no further action is required, and you have only invested a small amount of time. However, if the pattern continues, you now have evidence of what's occurred without having to rely on memory or vague recollections. You can present a specific record to the employee that will be hard for them to refute.

You're not wrong to think that maintaining documentation is building a case, but it's not limited to building cases for punitive or adverse actions. Positive employee actions should be equally documented and acknowledged. You could be building a case for employee advancement.

Question: Despite strong organizational values about treating each other with respect, one employee seems to enjoy engaging in controversial discussions—like politics—with coworkers. The problem is they do so in a very adversarial manner. It's getting to the point where our CEO wants to ban the discussion of certain topics completely. Is that a good idea, and, if not, how do we deal with the employee?

Answer: The topics aren't the problem, so banning them won't solve anything. The problem is the employee's conduct, so let's focus on how to address it.

Your organization's employee **conduct policy** likely has a **progressive discipline process** that starts with a discussion or verbal counseling. If you haven't already done so, have that discussion, letting the employee know exactly what you and others have observed, noting these observations have been frequent. Don't hesitate to mention that the CEO has taken notice. Most importantly, describe the impact the behavior is having on others, stressing that it has to change. Document this conversation.

If there is no change, move to the next stage, which is likely a **written disciplinary notice.** Such notices should include the date; the employee's name; the action being taken (for example, letter of caution or written notice); the specific issue or category of conduct (for example Disruptive Behavior); the specific behaviors observed and the dates they occurred; the impact of those behaviors or actions;

corrective actions and expectations of change; and a statement that if the employee fails to correct their behavior, further disciplinary action may be taken, up to and including termination.

Meet with the employee and review the disciplinary notice with them, pointing out the specific behaviors that have occurred since your first meeting. In both your written notice and your conversation, stick to the facts and avoid drawing conclusions or speculation, such as *I think you do these things because. . . .* Give the employee the opportunity to respond and ask if they have any questions. Once again, document the conversation noting that the employee did receive the disciplinary notice.

Continue to monitor the behavior. If it doesn't improve, it's time to confer with your leadership, HR, and possibly your legal advisors regarding next steps. A well-written and defensible policy will allow management flexibility to skip steps in the process depending on the severity of the behavior.

As hard as these discussions can be, remember that your organization is committed to a respectful workplace. You can't allow one employee to create a barrier to that goal.

Question: I have an employee who always wants to do things their way. When someone offers advice and guidance, or points out the correct way to do something, they respond by saying *sure*, then ignore it. Coworkers are complaining because this employee's lack of regard for standards and processes are impacting their jobs. How can I handle this situation?

Answer: Is this a matter of the employee can't change or won't change. Rather than focus on which, let's start with addressing the performance gap that exists. Employees are always accountable for their work performance, but there can be other factors that interfere.

As a manager, ask yourself the following:

- Were the work assignments and my expectations clear?
- Were the standards and process clearly explained?

- Did I provide sufficient support?
- Was the training the employee received adequate?
- Was I available to the employee?

Assuming the answers are yes, and there are no other intervening factors, this employee is likely solely accountable for this performance issue. It's time for a **performance improvement plan** or PIP. Implementing a PIP is not a negative action. They are meant to address and correct performance gaps.

In this case, the PIP can begin by explaining the standards for the task or tasks that the employee usually performs in their role. Next, list several tasks that will need to be completed correctly, describing how they will be completed (according to the standards) and how the results will be measured. Results can be measured in time, accuracy, quality, or impact on the tasks of coworkers. Finally, PIPs usually have time parameters included. For this situation, you may state that over the next thirty days, tasks are expected to be completed as described.

After thirty days, it's time to follow up and see if progress has been made. Assuming it has, let the employee know you will still be monitoring their job performance. You don't want them to revert to their bad habits.

However, if it's a matter of the employee won't change, it may also be a behavior issue. Performance and behavior issues can occur simultaneously. If that's the case, you can take disciplinary action at the same time as well. (Refer to the last question.) As you go down each path of management action, be clear with each what you're addressing: performance with the PIP and behavior with disciplinary notices.

Question: I've got a real quandary. Recently an investigation into workplace wrongdoing was conducted by our employment attorneys. Following their advice, we took action in accordance with our policies. Now, the employee who made the complaint is inquiring about the outcome, wanting to know specifics—what was found, what action was taken—and to review the investigation report that the attorney provided. What should I tell them?

Answer: I'm sure your attorney advised that the report they prepared is protected by **attorney-client privilege**, which is very common. Even if you had conducted an **internal investigation** with no legal guidance, the investigation report is still confidential. In either case, you are under no obligation to disclose it.

What to tell the employee? Tell them the report is the property of the organization, not part of their personnel file, and it contains confidential information, such as statements from witnesses or other information or documents that were part of the investigation. Make it clear they are not entitled to read all this information since it could taint the integrity of the investigation process. Pose the question: *Would you be willing to provide information in an investigation if the complaining party could read what you said?*

Regarding the employee's request to know about the action taken, once again stress **confidentiality** of the other employees involved. In these times when employees are expecting **transparency,** they need to realize that transparency is a two-way street. Pose this challenge: *Okay, I'll let you read the documents that explain what happened with your colleague; but if your behavior is the subject of an investigation, are you prepared for your personnel file to be opened to other curious employees?*

The best way to bring closure is to explain that a thorough investigation was conducted and based on the findings (and recommendations, if received from an external investigator) appropriate action was taken in accordance with policy. However, you cannot provide further, specific details. Thank the employee for bringing the matter to your attention, and request that if they become aware of continued issues, to please report them.

Question: I followed the advice in your last question. However, the employee won't accept the results of the investigation and is insisting that we missed something. To make it worse, they are continuing to bring additional, unrelated situations forward that are based solely on hearsay or their own observations, which they have not verified. I suspect they are talking with others and looking for problems that simply don't exist. Their behavior is starting to be disruptive. How do I address it?

Answer: People often draw conclusions on what they see without gathering all the facts—they are not seeing clearly. Sounds like this may be happening with your employee. Unfortunately, people project their own **assumptions and beliefs** on a situation without really knowing or seeing the reality of what's occurring.

A factor at the root of this problem is **confirmation bias**—why people easily accept information that aligns with their existing world views. People's beliefs can be influenced or distorted by emotion (such as fear or resentment), anxiety, their own self-perception and insecurities, and what they already believe. In addition, a person's individual diversity characteristics (such as ethnicity, age, education, and cultural variables, for example), and past experiences also shape beliefs and perceptions.

Of course, you can't get into this individual's thoughts and experiences to thoroughly understand why they think and feel the way they do. What you can do is address the behavior. Let the employee know the following:

- A trained and experienced investigator was engaged and that their **investigation** results have been reviewed and accepted.
- If they have facts that are relevant to the initial complaint, you are open to further consideration.
- You cannot accept hearsay, and you cannot accept observations that have not been substantiated (for example, there were no witnesses) as the reason for reopening an old investigation or starting a new one.
- Point out that while they may see a situation a certain way, other people may have different perceptions.

Finally, from what you describe, the employee is likely preventing others from doing their jobs and is likely not getting their own job done. You can address both the **behavior and performance deficiency** in accordance with your organization's policies, and you should not hesitate to do so.

Question: I was recently promoted and now have responsibility for two departments. When I first became a manager, I made the transition from peer to manager with just a few bumps. Now I'm hearing that some of my newer staff are disappointed with me. They had expected me to be more of a *buddy boss*. Should I change anything in my management style to meet these expectations?

Answer: It sounds as if you're making a good transition from **peer to manager**, so before you start adjusting your management and work style, give serious consideration to what's been working well and how you overcame those early bumps you experienced.

One of the most important things a successful manager needs to do is set **boundaries** with their team. That doesn't mean you can't socialize at work functions or outings nor participate in occasional lunches out of the office, but establishing close, social relationships with people you're responsible for supervising can create problems you likely don't want. For example, consider having to address the poor performance of an employee whom you see socially and how awkward that could be for both of you. Worse yet, what if you had to deliver news of a layoff to a *friend?* Conversely, if one of your employees is a constant tennis partner and you spend time together outside work, there could be the perception and accusations of favoritism.

Another potential trap of being a *buddy boss,* is the possibility of learning personal information about a team member—information that could bias a decision that you have to make regarding that employee. Successful managers have to be consistent in the way they make decisions and apply the organization's policies.

Setting boundaries doesn't mean you have to be aloof in your interactions with employees, nor does it mean you can't organize team events so everyone can have some light-hearted fun from time to time. However, it does mean roles and responsibilities must be clearly defined, and your behavior must reflect your role as a manager.

Finally, keep in mind, the workplace is a community, and all communities need leaders. Your role as a manager is to lead. That's the expectation you must live up to.

Question: One of my employees has been missing deadlines, and I'm getting reports that they have been ignoring requests from coworkers. This is out of character for them, and I suspect they are dealing with personal problems. I want to address these issues and offer some help through our Employee Assistance Program (EAP), but I'm not sure where to begin. Any suggestions?

Answer: It's good that you recognize this change in your employee's performance and behavior and want to offer help. The **Employee Assistance Program** can often stabilize a situation before it grows worse. Making referrals to the EAP can be difficult for a manager, but remember the EAP can help assess the situation and assist you with making the referral, including talking with the employee.

Be prepared to describe the specific behaviors and performance issues to both the EAP professional and the employee. This breaks through any denial that a problem exists. For example:

- *Over the past six weeks, you've missed these deadlines (give specifics), which caused delays in the project.*
- *On Monday, you were asked by (coworker) for certain files, and several others heard you say, "You'll get them when you get them."*

When confronting the employee, remember you are not a therapist or social worker. Leave diagnosing the root of the problem to the professionals. Focus on the productivity of your department. In talking with the employee:

- Let the employee know specific actions expected and deadlines for them, if applicable. Advise that if change does not happen, further action will be taken.

- Document the conversation.
- Initiate any management action in accordance with your policies.
- Make a management referral to the EAP, advising that the referral is voluntary. Stress that it's a resource to help improve the situation.
- Emphasize that the EAP is not a safe harbor, meaning that the employee remains accountable for their behavior.

Remember that a management referral to the EAP is voluntary. No punitive action can result if the employee fails to contact the EAP, and no conditions can be placed on the referral.

You will likely receive confirmation that the employee has or has not contacted the EAP. Feedback regarding the employee's progress depends on whether they authorized the EAP to contact you. Nevertheless, once the referral has been made, continue to observe, monitor, evaluate, and document the employee's performance, behavior, and progress. If there is no improvement, then further management action should be taken.

Question: We have a department with two people from the same family working together. Should I be concerned about this?

Answer: There are some things to be concerned about when an organization employs people from the same family, and some organizations have formal policies about the **employment of relatives**. The first is a breach of **confidentiality**. Be sure that there isn't the possibility that one employee has legitimate access, by nature of their job, to confidential information that might be shared with a family member that cannot have access to that information. **Scheduling** conflicts might also be an issue in the case of a family emergency when all family members would be absent at the same time. For example, you run a restaurant and your kitchen staff all are members of the same family. What happens if there is a death in the family and they all take time off for the funeral? Don't discount the fact that family issues and problems can also be brought to work leading to work-place drama and conflict.

It is never a good idea for a family member to have direct supervisory responsibility for another family member. The same can be said if one family member is in a certain staff position where one might have **approval authority** over actions involving the relative. For example, HR—approving or recommending decisions that could affect the relative, or accounting—approving requests for financial disbursements. In all these situations, there's the perception of favoritism and a perceived lack of objectivity. And confidentiality can once again be an issue. This is all fertile ground for potential conflict, or more seriously, **discrimination charges.**

When you are having a difficult time filling a specific position and someone recommends a member of their family who has the perfect skill set for the job, don't automatically reject the candidate. Carefully weigh the pros and cons and odds are you will make the right decision.

Question: An employee asked me if it would be all right if we took the team out on their boat as a team building activity. Was I wrong to say no?

Answer: No, you probably did the right thing, but let's talk about why saying no was correct.

This activity, fun as it sounds, would potentially put your organization at risk. Since they wanted it to be a **team-building event**, it can now become a company co-sponsored event.

- Will it occur during normal working hours?
- Who will be responsible for planning the event?
- Will there be alcohol available?
- Will there be food?
- Who will pay for any food, other refreshments, and gas for the boat?

- Who will plan and who will facilitate the team building portion of the event?
- Will there be activities other than team building, such as water skiing or paddle boarding?

This is not a simple goodwill gesture that allows a manager and all the team members to get to know each other better in an informal setting. It now has become an organization event presenting possible risks and costs. For example, if alcohol is consumed, coupled with the effects of being in the sun, there is an increased potential for injury. If anyone is injured, the organization will incur **workers compensation** claims and costs. Alcohol plus sun and fun can increase the possibility of **sexual harassment** behavior, raising the possibility of legal risks.

A better suggestion for a manager who seriously wants to build their team would be to work with them to schedule some events that everyone agrees on. These can be online or in person where activities are carefully planned. There can surely be fun built in, but the main purpose is for the staff to get to know and trust each other.

While you certainly can't prohibit the employee from inviting coworkers on their boat, making it a team building event is the issue. Your instincts as a manager were right to say no. Good for you.

Question: One of my colleagues mentioned that they keep a file on each of their direct reports. Is this something I should do and if so, what would I put in it? I send anything related to my employees to the HR department for their files. What is the best practice here?

Answer: Good for you for sending related employee documents to HR. That is where the official **employee file** is maintained.

I imagine what your colleague was referring to is commonly called a *working file*. This is where they probably put notes of conversations with their staff or maybe something personal like *Sally's son is playing Little League this year* so they can mention it to Sally during one of their meetings.

These types of notes and reminders are fine, but what isn't fine is keeping any kind of documentation on the employee's performance only in a file in the manager's desk. Such documentation needs to go immediately to HR to be included in the official personnel file. Here's why. Let's say that a manager puts **written documentation** of a serious mistake the employee made and how it is being resolved. Months later, what if that employee is up for a **promotion** and the hiring manager goes to HR and asks to review that employee's file? A key piece of information is missing.

The same thing could happen with positive information. If the manager shares something positive about an employee's actions or contribution and doesn't send a copy to HR, the hiring manager would miss out on a significant detail that might have moved the employee to the top of the list for the promotion.

Unfortunately, some managers think by keeping information to themselves, it will not be discoverable if there is ever any legal action. That is not true and in fact, it could make a situation worse if it was seen as the organization was trying to hide information.

So, keep doing what you're doing and forward any employee related information to HR. You will be doing the right thing and your HR team will thank you.

Question: One of our new employees asked to use an empty conference room for a prayer meeting with other colleagues. Is this a good idea?

Answer: If you allow other employees to use the conference room for nonwork events, yes, you should grant access to the group wanting to use it for prayer. Under **Title VII of the Civil Rights Act of 1964**, you must make a **reasonable accommodation** for an employee's religious beliefs provided it does not impose a serious hardship or interfere with business operations.

For example, you may grant permission to groups for book clubs to meet and if so, denying the request for the prayer group would be a violation of Title VII.

However, that said, you may want to come up with some guidelines for reserving the conference rooms for non-work-related events. For example:

- Room requests must be received at least forty-eight hours in advance to the appropriate staff member.
- Rooms must be used as is or returned to the way you found it. Facilities staff may not be used to reconfigure furniture.
- Rooms must be cleaned and any trash taken to the dumpster.
- A work-related event always supersedes a non-work-related event.

Another consideration, and be sure to find out the details before granting this or other requests: How frequently do they want to use the room? Will they meet every day, weekly, or monthly? Is this frequency realistic? Will it interfere with business operations?

It sounds as if this might not be a one-time request. If that's the case, what happens if and when there is a scheduling conflict? Obviously, if the room is needed for business purposes on a day this or any other group wants to meet, there needs to be a notification process in place. Make it clear to the group leader they are responsible for checking on the room's availability every time they want to use it. This will reduce conflict in the future.

NAVIGATING THE CHANGING WORKPLACE

Question: With more people working from home, many fully remote, we lack control over their work environment and home offices and can't physically inspect them. Since my team spends most of their days at computers, I'm concerned about injuries and physical stress. What can we do to minimize any injury and address potential workers compensation issues?

Answer: You make some excellent points in your question. To begin with, **workers compensation** laws are applied at the state level, so begin there to understand how at-home work applies to state laws. Check with your state(s)' workers compensation board, your insurance broker, or workers compensation carrier for current information.

You're right that employers don't have total control over a workers' home environments. For example, if they trip over a child's toy in the hallway and sprain their ankle, it's probably not a liability. If most of the staff are knowledge workers, they are vulnerable to repetitive stress injuries. There are several things an employer can do to address **ergonomics,** namely:

- Consider offering an allowance to purchase ergonomically safe equipment—desk and chair.
- Research this equipment and provide recommendations and guidance. You may even be able to negotiate employee discounts with certain companies.
- If a new employee has existing equipment, ask for proof that it meets sound, ergonomic standards.
- Provide online ergonomic training. This should be offered to everyone, but it's especially important for remote staff. There are private organizations and universities that offer online ergonomic training for remote workers.
- Conduct work-from-home ergonomic assessments or self-assessments. There are companies that offer these services, many of which do virtual assessments. It's a way to inspect at-home workspaces without an employer representative invading the privacy of an employee's home.
- Look for other resources online such as working from home ergonomic checklists.
- Encourage staff to move around, take breaks, and do simple exercises during their workday. It's one of the advantages of being out of the office—no one will see you doing yoga poses.

Coordinate your efforts with either internal team members or external consultants who advise you on human resources, legal, and risk management issues. Your insurance broker or workers compensation carrier may also have resources you can use.

Finally, make sure that all employees know the procedures for reporting any work-related injury. Even if they take all of the precautions that you recommend and follow all the guidelines you put in place, it doesn't mean you'll never have an employee who suffers an injury.

Question: Our organization, like most, has adopted policies around flexibility since the 2020 pandemic. However, some employees, all geographically close, are refusing to come into the office at all. How should we respond?

Answer: The workplace and the workforce has certainly changed since 2020 with new **business models** and ways of working, including **hybrid work arrangements** and flexibility emerging. Before responding to these employees, examine the following questions that could explain their resistance:

- Have you asked them about their reluctance to return, even occasionally? For example, are there workplace-specific stressors not consciously identified before that they now dread having to deal with? If you haven't asked yet, do so now.
- What is the nature of the work these employees perform? Are they finding there are too many interruptions at work? If they can be more productive at home, consider if their presence in the office is necessary.
- Are employees coming into the office, only to spend the day on Zoom or in other virtual meetings with no face-to-face interactions with their coworkers?
- Has your organization put appropriate procedures in place to address health and safety concerns?

Assuming your organization has addressed these issues, then consider how often you would like these employees to be in the office and how you can incentivize them to do so.

Stress the importance of building and maintaining relationships with their peers, especially if your organization focuses on team-based results. Explain that periodic, face-to-face meetings help to attain this goal.

Consider holding scheduled, periodic meetings, perhaps one day a week or every other week, as a way to begin. Another alternative is to require meetings only for specific events—at the start of a new project, for project reviews, or for brainstorming sessions—rather than on a scheduled basis. In either case, don't require them to stay in the office all day. Once the meeting is over, they are free to go. If it's really necessary for them to be in the office periodically, can it be for a shorter period of time, perhaps 10:00 am to 3:00 pm? Whatever approach you take, don't overstep the requirement to be present.

Question: We recently disciplined an employee who had been posting extremely negative comments about the organization on external chat boards and other social media platforms. After refusing to stop the behavior, their response was that freedom of speech was their *God-given, First Amendment right,* and the organization could not limit what they said about anything. Are they correct?

Answer: Let's take a look at what the **First Amendment** of the Constitution says about **Freedom of Speech**. "Congress shall make no law . . . abridging the freedom of speech, or of the press." What does this mean today? No government agency—federal, state, or local—or officials—legislative, executive, or judicial—may restrict or punish an individual for what they say or write, except in exceptional circumstances. It does not extend these protections to private individuals or organizations, such as private employers.

The First Amendment restrains only the government, so it appears that you have not violated the rights of this employee for taking disciplinary action, unless you are a government agency.

Consider some other situations where employers have rightfully restricted speech in the workplace. Employers have an obligation to maintain workplaces free of **harassment and discrimination**. If employees verbally abuse coworkers with derogatory remarks, insults, and epithets, or if they reduce this behavior to writing, they are going to be disciplined.

Employers also have the obligation to maintain workplaces that are safe and free from harm. If employees threaten or intimidate coworkers, or make **threats of violence**, that behavior will not be tolerated, and employees will be disciplined.

Finally, organizations have an interest in maintaining their reputations in their communities. It's important that the values and culture of the organization are accurately reflected. It sounds as if this is the situation you are facing—inaccurate portrayal of the organization. Unfortunately, social media and other communication platforms challenge organizations' efforts in this area.

Organizations can, and have, taken action to address this type of behavior. Of course, it's advisable to speak with your legal counsel or team and review all of the particulars of this situation before taking any further action with this employee.

Question: Using your gender pronouns in your signature, social media accounts, and on video calls is becoming the norm. Some of my colleagues are bewildered by this practice and reluctant to do so. Can you provide some insight so I can help my colleagues understand the importance of doing so?

Answer: You can't always know what someone's pronouns are by looking at them or by their name. **Gender pronouns** are the terms people choose to refer to themselves that reflect their **gender identity,** and many people identify outside the binary of male/female. Using a gender-neutral or gender-inclusive pronoun does not associate a binary gender (male or female) to the individual.

Gender-neutral pronouns are also useful when you don't know the gender of the person you're talking about—the person who made the delivery or a person from another culture with an unfamiliar name.

People's names and pronouns are personal, and using them properly shows respect. Would you consider calling someone by a nickname that they didn't agree to or like just because it's a common nickname for their given name?

So, it is important to know and use a person's correct pronouns. It fosters inclusion, makes people feel valued, and affirms their gender identity. Using the wrong pronoun can make them feel invalidated, dismissed, or alienated, which can go against your best **diversity and inclusion** efforts.

Societal changes can be challenging. There are things that you can do to incorporate these changes and help others accept them. As more people share their pronouns, even individuals who identify as male or female, the practice becomes more familiar and puts more people at ease.

When you introduce yourself to new colleagues, share your pronouns: *My name is Chris, and I go by he/him.* Take it a step further: *What pronouns do you use?* If you don't know someone's gender pronouns, simply ask what their pronouns are or how they would like to be referred to. Finally, if someone uses an incorrect pronoun referring to a colleague, gently and gracefully correct them. *In case you didn't know, Randy uses they/them pronouns.*

Much of this change is about shifting our habits and getting past the old rules of grammar we've been taught. You've made a good first step in recognizing the need to help others make this shift.

Question: So much of the talk about hybrid and remote work has been focused on where the work is performed. Most of our employees have the flexibility of working from home, if not every day, at least the majority of the time. I've been made aware that many employees often use their own personal equipment—computers and other devices—because their equipment is technically better. Should we be allowing employees to use their own devices?

Answer: To help you make the best decision for your organization, because there's no right answer, let's look at **technology use** in today's environment.

There are risks and advantages of employees using their **personal computers and devices** for work. Your organization should be considering the following:

Do you know what devices your employees are using? Even if they are given computers and/or tablets, they may be defaulting to using their own because they are, in the employee's opinions, superior. This would be a good time to ask them. With a simple poll, you can find out if they are using employer-issued equipment and tools, their own technology that the organization has approved, or equipment and tools you know nothing about.

Did you discover that a majority of your employees are using personal technology? If so, this would be a good time to invest in technology upgrades, if necessary. This investment allows your organization to enable the latest **data security software** and features that secure your sensitive data. Be certain you can provide the appropriate technical support for installation and maintenance of equipment and software you provide.

If employees are using personal equipment and devices because from their perspective, they will be more productive, both employers and employees need to weigh increased productivity against the following:

- Employees may be entitled to reimbursement for technology tools and in some cases for their internet and phone connections. Don't overlook subscription services they might also be using. Certain state laws address this requirement, and it's often the employee's location, not where the organization is based, that triggers the requirement.
- There could be security implications for employees who are using their own devices. The employer might require certain software to be installed which could compromise their personal data.
- Employers have security concerns as well. Are employee's personal networks secure? Are there encryption protocols in place?

Best practice is for managers, the leadership, and your **IT support** to come together to discuss the resources you have, your ability to manage those resources, and the best way to ensure a productive workforce.

Question: My organization does not have a policy that restricts dating nor any requirement for employees to report to HR when they are in a consensual romantic relationship. I thought these policies and requirements were necessary. Am I wrong?

Response: After the #MeToo movement of 2017, many organizations did review their **sexual harassment prevention policies**, especially around **consensual romantic relationships**, and made changes. Some implemented requirements regarding reporting such romantic involvements to HR, while others imposed dating restrictions, which frankly, don't often work. Let's look at these issues closer.

There is a potential danger if members of leadership, or even managers, are dating individuals who are in their sphere of management influence (or chain of command). There are many high-profile cases of executives stepping down or being terminated because of this very situation. It's not unreasonable for organizations to prohibit (or restrict) these types of consensual relationships. They open the door to claims of sexual harassment and/or the perception of favoritism.

For organizations that do want to prohibit relationships between managers and their employees, they need to be aware that there could be challenges if they require the resignation or transfer of the *subordinate employee,* especially if that employee is a female or member of another protected class. If opportunities are taken away or diminished, the employee may have a claim of discrimination.

Relationships among coworkers or peers, however, is a different situation. They do hold the potential for workplace disruption and/or claims of harassment, especially when one individual ends the relationship, and that is a reason to be concerned.

Having a requirement to report consensual relationships to HR is not a guarantee that problems will be avoided, and HR does have more to do than monitor these relationships.

As a manager, there are some things you can do. First is to be proactive about your organization's **harassment policy.** Make sure your team is aware of it, and take the time to discuss it in meetings, including its complaint procedures. Pay attention to workplace conduct and immediately address behavior that is not professionally appropriate according to your policies. Even though you can't prevent office romances from occurring, you can manage employees' workplace behavior.

Question: In recent years there seems to be an increase in union activity, much of which is occurring in industries like warehousing and retail. Some of my colleagues think that because of our industry, we're immune from unionizing attempts and employee activism. Are they right and are there things managers need to know?

Answer: While union organizing activity did grow in certain industries over issues related to pay and safe working conditions, especially related to the 2020 pandemic, no industry is immune.

Under the **National Labor Relations Act, or NLRA,** all employees have the right to organize, form, join, assist, and be represented by a union, to bargain collectively through representatives of their own choosing, and to engage in concerted activity, for example discussing terms and conditions of employment, such as their salaries or task assignments.

If the employees are engaged in **union organizing,** or concerted activities, managers should avoid taking actions that could be considered an **unfair labor practice.** These actions include eavesdropping on conversations (spying), claiming the union will lower wages and force the organization to take away benefits and opportunities (threats), asking employees about union activities (interrogation), and suggesting benefits such as salary increases if employees vote against a union or refrain from union activities (promises). Any actions that could be retaliation or perceived as retaliatory should also be avoided.

Union organizing usually follows the **National Labor Relations Board's** process: an organizing campaign, signed authorization cards, a petition for certification, election campaigns, and elections where a union is or is not elected by the employees in the bargaining unit. However, recognition of a bargaining unit may occur under other circumstances, such as a union convincing the employer to grant recognition or a union convincing an employer to witness its majority status.

Beyond traditional union activity, other forms of **employee activism** have also evolved in recent years. Platforms such as Zoom allow an opportunity for union organizing activities outside of the workplace. On Coworker.org, employees can conduct crowdsource campaigns to pressure organizations to treat workers better in terms of pay, safety, and benefits, a practice that allows for the expansion of employee activism.

If managers suspect any union organizing activity, or any other form of employee activism, they should alert senior management, legal counsel, and/or HR immediately.

AVOIDING LEGAL PITFALLS

Question: In a conversation I had recently with an employee who supports our team, but doesn't work directly for me, it came out that she has been experiencing harassment by a member of the leadership team. She told me she's handling it and does not want anything done. I want to keep her confidentiality, but I'm not sure saying nothing is the best course to take. Did I handle this appropriately? Should I have another conversation with her?

Answer: Maintaining employee confidentiality is critical, except in certain circumstances—and this is one of them. As a manager, if you have knowledge of **sexual harassment** or other forms of harassment, you have an obligation to report it. However, before doing so, you should definitely have another conversation with the employee. Here are some things to keep in mind as you approach that conversation:

1. First, explain your responsibility as a manager to take action and report it to the appropriate party in the organization, likely Human Resources. Let the employee know that you don't have a choice.
2. Next, ask the employee specifically what she's doing to "handle it." If she's using avoidance tactics, explain that won't be effective in the long run. The only way to stop the behavior is to address it. It's important that she understands that if the individual has a visible role in the organization, their behavior is likely affecting others. Stress that this is not good for all the employees nor the work environment.
3. Finally, encourage her to come with you to report the issue. Explain that sooner or later an investigation will have to take place. If HR hears the details of the harassing behavior directly from the employee, the investigation will have a solid start.

Throughout the conversation, be empathetic and supportive. Acknowledge the employee's concerns about potential retaliation, and let her know you understand that it is not comfortable having to make this type of report, but neither is being the subject of continued harassment. Emphasize the organization's commitment to a respectful work environment that is free of harassment of any kind.

Question: Our company has a PTO policy that allows employees to take time off for personal or health reasons. One of my staff members recently gave me two days' notice that they needed time off with no reason provided. I was short staffed during that time, so I asked if it was for health-related reasons thinking I could spare them for a day or two if it was. They said it was for a prescheduled, personal event. Was I wrong asking about the reason under the circumstances?

Answer: Organizations used to have separate categories of **paid time off**—sick days and vacation days. In those systems, it was easier to understand the reason for the request, with no worries about being invasive.

Let's look at some of the potential concerns in your question. It sounds as if you asked a general question about the reason for the time off, "Is it health related or not?" As long as you weren't delving into the nature of a potential health reason, you likely weren't skirting any violation of the **Americans with Disabilities Act.**

Time off for health-related reasons could be covered by the **Family Medical Leave Act,** in which case the employer has obligations to provide certain notices to the employee and ensure they are receiving all of their benefits under the law. This would support your asking about the nature of the requested time off.

As a manager, you have a responsibility to make sure that all of the team's work gets done. If you were short staffed, you were likely concerned about added burden to the rest of the team. If the employee had a prescheduled, personal event, two days' notice does not seem very reasonable nor considerate to their coworkers. You may want to implement procedures for time-off requests, if they don't already exist, and discuss them with your team at a future staff meeting.

Question: Recently an employee brought to my attention an unfortunate comment that was made in a meeting that the employee claimed targeted a coworker who was a person of color. I later learned the speaker apologized and the apology was accepted. I'd like to discuss microaggressions in our next staff meeting. Is this a good idea, and how should I introduce the topic?

Answer: Yes, it's a very good idea. **Microaggressions** are receiving more attention, and employees are more aware of them. They are biased comments and actions taken often against people of color, women, workers with disabilities, and other protected groups. They are indirect and subtle, and they can be hard to recognize.

Oftentimes, microaggressions are not intentional. Someone may make a comment without thinking and realize after the fact that it might have had an adverse effect on someone else. It sounds as if that's what happened in your situation. Intentional or not, microaggressions can cause harm and, left unchecked, they can lead to bigger problems like discrimination or harassment claims.

How can you have this conversation with your team? Here are some ideas:

- Describe what microaggressions are and provide examples. Simply, they are unprofessional behavior (such as taking someone's ideas and presenting them as your own) or demeaning comments (such as referring to women as girls thereby implying they are not equal contributors).
- Describe the negative impact they can have on the workplace. They alienate employees and potential hires. They can ruin working relationships and force valued talent out the door. They negatively impact the workplace environment and everyone's productivity.
- Describe the organization's commitment, and your personal commitment, for ensuring a respectful and an inclusive workplace. This is an opportunity to review your values along with policies that support those values.

Starting this conversation is a good first step, and you need to keep it up if you want to maintain a culture of respect and inclusion. Let your employees know that you are committed to hearing their complaints and addressing any problems they identify. Then, take those complaints seriously if you receive them, and get your HR and legal teams involved, especially if the behavior becomes more serious. In other words, take action and lead by example.

Finally, discuss with your leadership the idea of including the topic of microaggressions into management training and any anti-harassment training the organization offers. In addition, a message from the top leader in your organization is also effective in letting employees know this behavior will not be tolerated.

Question: The information in the last question was very helpful, especially about adding microaggressions as a topic in management and anti-harassment training. I'm wondering, though, if training is enough. Are there other things that managers can do beside just having conversations with their staff?

Answer: I'm so glad you asked this question, and yes, there are other things that managers can do to support a positive **workplace culture**.

We often focus entirely on negative behavior, such as calling out **microaggressions** as a preventative measure. That's an entirely reactive approach. While it's important that such behavior is not ignored and should be addressed, also consider taking a proactive approach as well.

Catch people doing things right and celebrate their actions, such as treating a coworker with respect. In other words, when you see someone doing something positive, call that out as well. For example, you've witnessed or been told that one team member went out of their way to help a coworker who was struggling with something. Find an appropriate way to acknowledge the individual and their actions. It can be a simple *shout out* in a staff meeting or a message to the team.

For those employees who speak up about behavior that does not support the organization's culture and values, be sure to acknowledge them as well. This may require a more subtle or less public approach, but acknowledge their actions, nevertheless.

How do you do that and institutionalize such practices within the organization? One approach is to introduce **bystander intervention training**. People often want to help, but are unsure how and what to do. Intervention is a skill that can be developed with practice, and such training introduces a number of techniques to do so.

A culture where being open and encouraging feedback from employees doesn't happen overnight. You can do your part by creating feedback loops, listening carefully to what your employees tell you, acting on the best information you have, and letting your employees know how much you value them and the information they provide. One of the most important things you can do is to let your employees know how much they helped create your organization's success and their own security and future.

Question: I'm new to my current employer, and one of my team members has been asking about their employment contract. A former coworker apparently has been talking about their new employment contract and reading about them in employment advice columns. My employee is also hinting that the former manager made certain promises and guarantees about their employment situation. I've never worked in an organization that had employment contracts. Is there something I'm missing?

Answer: Let's unbundle these issues. First, the majority of states in this country have **employment-at-will** laws, which means that with certain exceptions, such as discriminatory reasons, an employer can hire and fire workers with or without cause.

Second, while **employment contracts** do exist, generally for high-ranking executives or union-represented employees, most U.S. employees are not covered by these formal contracts. Certainly, if your current employer used employment contracts, you would have been told about them and asked to sign one.

It is hard to know the exact terms and conditions of employment this former colleague may be experiencing in their new job. It could be they were asked to sign a noncompete agreement, a nondisclosure agreement, an assignment (to the employer) of certain rights for work products developed in the course of employment, or something else. These are not the same as individual employment contracts.

Unfortunately, it's easy to use, or misuse, terms like employment contract, especially in the public press, where most employment advice columns reside. Unless the writer of the column is an employment lawyer, don't get too concerned.

The most pressing issue you appear to be facing is the allegation of certain promises and guarantees about employment that were made. These types of comments could erode your organization's employment-at-will policy. For example, if a statement similar to *as long as your performance meets standards, you'll have a job here* was made, it could be an indication of an **implied contract**, which is another exception to the employment-at-will doctrine.

Talk with the employee to find out exactly what the former manager said, document the conversation, and contact your HR and legal teams right away for advice. While you're speaking with them, ask what actions, if any, they suggest you take to address this issue if it arises in the future.

CLOSING THOUGHTS

As a manager, you have probably realized that the answer to every people issue that comes your way won't be found in the policy manual. There should be resources, internal or external, that can help you. Get to know who and what those resources are, and develop relationships with the appropriate staff, such as your HR and legal teams, so they can help you resolve problems. Admittedly, some will never be pleasant or easy, but never feel you are on your own.

SECTION 6

ENSURING GRACEFUL ENDINGS

IT DOESN'T MATTER how well we manage our organizations, there may be a time when you need to lay off staff or to terminate an employee for cause—either for nonperformance or conduct. Sometimes employees choose to leave. Whatever the circumstances, you'll want to make the situation as painless as possible. Some of the strategies in this section are around planning for a layoff or a termination, the importance of exit interviews, and how to ensure the employees who remain in the organization understand what happened and feel as good as possible about it.

Graceful endings are a fact of life and while no one enjoys participating in them, when handled with care, your organization will be stronger than ever.

Question: We have given an employee every opportunity to improve their performance, but to no avail. It's time to terminate them, and I need tips on what I should be doing and how and when I should be doing it. Can you help?

Answer: I am sorry it has come to this. It would have been great if the employee had improved their performance so that you didn't have to take this action.

First, consider the following:

- Did you set clear expectations about **employee performance**, and did the employee understand them?
- Are these conversations documented?
- Did you provide counseling, coaching, mentoring, or other means to help the employee improve their performance and are these actions documented?
- Have you reviewed the termination with your leadership including HR, and do you have their approval and support?
- Is there a need to seek any legal advice, and if so, have you done so?

Once you are ready to proceed, do your best to have the **termination meeting** in person, unless the employee is remote. Have someone—your HR representative or another manager—in the meeting to witness what transpires. Make notes immediately after the meeting regarding what was said.

When you meet with the employee, get to the point quickly. Review your past discussions and any relevant documentation. Prepare a script in advance so you know exactly what you want to say.

While there is no perfect time to terminate someone, it makes sense to meet with the individual late in the day, especially if most of the staff works in the office. Taking the action early in the week, preferably on a Monday, allows the employee to start a job search immediately.

Finally, coordinate with other departments who have administrative roles to play. For example:

- HR will need to prepare a termination letter outlining benefit information, such as COBRA or any severance being offered; the confidential nature of termination information; non-compete details; and other relevant information.
- IT needs to be advised to turn off the employee's network access.
- Facilities, or another department, needs to arrange for the return of property.

Good luck with your planning and the action you are taking. Remember to rely on your HR team and legal counsel if necessary.

Question: We have an arrangement with a temporary placement firm. Sometimes they place individuals for limited-term assignments. At other times, the placement will be a temp-to-perm arrangement. We have an employee currently in a temp-to-perm arrangement, and the individual just isn't working out. How do I tell her that we no longer need her services, and how do we get company property (keys, etc.) back from her?

Answer: If you are working through a **temporary placement firm**, you shouldn't do anything other than let the agency know the person isn't working out. It is up to them to let the individual know not to return to work. It should be the responsibility of the agency to get keys or any of your company property back and return it to you. This should include passwords as well as parking passes or anything else that is specific to your organization.

Before you tell them to have the ending conversation, work out the timing so that they have a replacement ready to start work when you need them.

This may be a time to review the placement agency you are currently using so that you have the best pool of candidates. Talk with your current agency, and research additional agencies. If you do decide to make a change, you need to plan ahead as to when to let the first agency know you won't be continuing to use their service.

Bottom line, one of the advantages of using an agency is you don't have to terminate a nonperforming staffer.

Question: Unfortunately, the leadership in my organization has made the decision that we must reduce staff. All managers were advised to begin assessing their team members so we can make recommendations. I've never had to do this, and I'm really uncomfortable. How do I choose employees for a layoff?

Answer: Layoffs, unfortunately, occur in organizations for a number of different reasons. What you're describing is not unusual—the need for an organization to reduce costs, including labor costs. Having to make these types of selection decisions are certainly not easy.

Start with looking at the work your team performs. Are there any functions that are not necessary or that could be combined? This allows you to look at positions first and individuals second. It's the beginning of your needs assessment.

While you're looking at functions, consider **skills**. What skills are necessary to perform these functions you identified? Consider:

- What does your team look like today—functions and skills?
- What will it need to look like after the layoff to be successful?
- What knowledge, skills, and abilities (KSAs) will be needed?
- Are there certain **positions** that can be eliminated?

Now that you are more comfortable with the needs of your department to perform the necessary work, you can begin to turn your attention to the people. Apply the following objective criteria as you continue your assessment.

- Who on the team possesses those necessary KSAs?
- What is each individual's performance history?
- What is each individual's reliability and employment history?
- What is each individual's length of service?

Hopefully, your organization's leadership, including HR, has provided some insights and guidance for the particulars of this situation. For example, if you think two people possess similar skills, knowledge, performance history, and reliability records, the one with the least amount of seniority should be chosen for layoff.

When you present your recommendations, be sure you can support them. This means having appropriate documentation. Remember, you're making a business case—one that affects the lives of individuals.

Question: My organization conducts exit interviews when employees leave, and I've often wondered what purpose they serve. Does it make sense to conduct exit interviews and, if so, how and when is the right time to conduct them?

Answer: Yes, it is a good idea to talk to exiting employees, especially those who leave voluntarily. People who voluntarily leave can provide you with insights you won't get anywhere else. Obviously, you shouldn't do an **exit interview** with an employee you terminated for cause or even those who are laid off due to lack of work. The responses you'll get from them will likely be negative and emotional because of the circumstances.

Your sole purpose in asking for exit data is to learn information that will help you improve your operation, including each department's operation. Keep that in mind as you plan your process.

Consider doing the exit interview on or near the last day of employment. If possible, have the interview conducted by an outside consultant or by someone in the HR department. They are likely to be more objective than the employee's direct supervisor who is more connected with the individual. The employee will probably not give you the information you seek if their direct supervisor is doing the interview.

Some organizations have success with doing exit interviews six months or so after people leave. They feel they get better information after the employee has had time to process why they left and when all financial connections to your organizations have ended. At this point, they will have been paid anything owed to them and will have had their 401(k) accounts moved where they want them, so they feel more comfortable being honest with you about how you could improve your organization.

Some organizations use a survey to collect exit information. While this can be effective and it's easy to tabulate the results, most organizations find the return rate of the form to be low.

As with any survey or employee information you collect, be sure to analyze and use the data. If you begin to see patterns of turnover in certain departments, this is when action can be taken. However, if everyone who leaves your organization complains about a particular policy or everyone from a particular department complains about a particular manager, you'll want to move as quickly as possible to make necessary changes or look into the situation.

Question: Should everyone be asked the same questions in an exit interview, or should they be varied? What types of questions are typically asked, and what defense does a manager have if an employee provides negative information?

Answer: Let's take each issue separately. First, it is best to create a list of questions for the **exit interview** that you ask of everyone who voluntarily leaves. Asking the same questions of everyone ensures consistency, guards against bias, and allows the organization to look for trends.

Here are some typical questions that have been shown to be effective:

- What is your primary reason for leaving us?
- Did anything specific trigger your decision to leave?
- Is there anything we could have done to retain you?
- What would you have changed about your job if you could have?
- Do you have a new job, and, if so, did they offer you something you couldn't get here? Is your salary higher? Do they offer benefits we don't offer?
- What suggestions do you have for making our organization a better place to work?
- When you were hired, was your onboarding process effective? If no, how could we improve?
- Will you refer friends and colleagues to us? Why or why not?
- If the circumstances were right, would you consider returning to work here?
- Is there anything we haven't asked you that you'd like to share?

Finally, you asked about a manager's defense if an individual employee provides negative information. While it may be tempting to take one person's comments and run with them, it is advisable to wait until more data has been collected before acting on a single exit interview. It's why we said in the last question to look for trends. That one interview with negative comments may be an outlier. In that case, it would not be unreasonable to follow up with a manager about some negative comments. It's an opportunity to gain a different perspective.

Question: We are planning a layoff. I think we have a solid strategy for taking good care of the people we will be losing, but I am concerned about the impact on the remaining employees. Can you provide some tips to keep in mind for those employees who are staying with us?

Answer: This is such a key issue and one that many organizations overlook when planning a layoff. In some respects, it is as critical to your success as how you handle the people who unfortunately will be leaving in the layoff.

Communication and sensitivity are keys when dealing with **employees who remain after a layoff.** You want to, as best you can, control the information that is shared. Keep in mind your staff will be impacted and will likely be thinking:

- Who will pick up the work of the laid-off staffers?
- Are there more layoffs planned, and will I be impacted?
- Were my former coworkers and my friends treated well?

Consider preparing a script for all managers to follow when addressing questions such as these. The script should contain truthful information that can be shared and, if appropriate, include information on where employees can find additional information.

The script should direct managers not to make up their own answers. If asked a question not covered in the script, they can say,

"Great question and I am not the one to answer that. Contact HR, please."

Some managers have trouble admitting they can't answer a question, but it is really important to remind them to keep to the script so that they don't say something that could cause harm down the road.

It is a good idea to hold an all hands meeting as soon as the layoffs are completed. The CEO or other leader should stress how important the remaining staff is to the organization and show empathy for those who left and those who stay. It's important not to make any promises that can't be kept but to reassure the staff that they are valuable to the organization.

Treat the remaining staff with care, and remember that many of them may be suffering because they won't be working with someone who was more than a coworker—they were a friend. Be honest, but of course, don't share any confidential information you may have. Most importantly, remind them that they have an important role to play, show them you value them, and treat them with respect.

AVOIDING LEGAL PITFALLS

Question: I'm new to my management role, and, in the past, I've been aware of employees being fired. Sometimes when that happened, there was a great deal of speculation about whether or not termination was fair. Before I terminate an employee for cause, what should I consider so I'm not putting my organization at legal risk?

Answer: Likely your organization has policies addressing **terminations for cause,** which are usually because of poor performance or the violation of work rules, policies, or procedures.

Work with your HR team to make sure you understand the policies and the procedures for **corrective discipline** and/or **performance improvement.** Before you present your recommendation to terminate an employee, examine the situation and consider the following:

1. If a policy was violated, was the violation serious? Did it impact others?

2. How have similar violations been handled in the past? Has my department been consistent following policy in handling past violations?
3. How long has the employee worked here?
4. Has the employee been involved with policy violations in the past?
5. What is the employee's performance history?
6. Has the employee had the opportunity to correct their behavior or improve their performance?
7. Are there mitigating circumstances to consider?
8. Have any federal, state, or local laws been violated that require specific action?
9. If claims of harassment or discrimination been made, have the claims been thoroughly investigated by the appropriate parties? Has all the evidence been examined?
10. Have I reviewed all of my documentation and given the employee the opportunity to change their behavior or performance?

Then, ask yourself the following:

- Am I comfortable with the facts?
- Am I comfortable with the evidence supporting the facts?
- Have I clearly documented the problem?
- Considering the employee's tenure and history, am I treating the employee with fairness and respect?
- Would terminating the employee now prevent vesting in benefits in the near future?
- Am I treating the employee like others in the same situation?
- Have I explored alternatives such as transfer, reassignment, or training?
- Can I defend my recommendation to terminate?

Question: It used to be easy to set workplace standards around expected behavior. However, social media and remote working

have changed relationships among employees and their relationship with their employer. Can employees be fired for behavior that occurred outside of work, especially if that behavior reflects poorly on the company?

Answer: Like so many answers you are likely to get from either your HR or your legal advisor, it depends on the circumstances. So, let's break it down in very general terms.

If your organization is an **at-will** employer, you probably have a statement or policy that says employees are free to join or leave *and* the organization is free to establish or end the employment relationships at any time with or without cause or notice. This is true as long as the employer's decision doesn't violate any of the exceptions to the **employment-at-will doctrine**, such as laws and regulations.

You mentioned social media. A question to consider: What was the employee (or employees) using social media for? Were they discussing working conditions? If so, it could be a protected concerted activity under the National Labor Relations Act and termination would be ill advised.

On the other hand, if an employee listed their employer in their profile and was posting discriminatory statements on a social media platform, yes, that could be a poor reflection on your organization. Also, it could potentially be creating a hostile work environment for other employees. What if the employee was breaching confidentiality or trade secret clauses? Termination in any of these instances could be justified.

Some laws provide protection to **whistleblowers** or employees who report illegal activity or workplace violations. There may also be state laws with broad protections covering **off-duty employee conduct** that you have to consider. For example, you may not be able to prevent an employee from outside employment, unless there is a conflict of interest.

Hopefully, you're beginning to see how complex these issues can be. Each situation must be evaluated separately, and it's critical to seek legal advice.

NAVIGATING THE CHANGING WORKPLACE

Question: An employee abruptly terminated their employment several months ago, leaving a significant gap in the team. They recently called to apologize and offered a vague explanation for their actions. I suspect they are trying to make amends because they need me as a reference. What should I say if I get a call asking about their employment?

Answer: In recent years, it's not been unusual for employees to leverage their options and be focused on what's best for them and their careers, unfortunately not thinking about the employer and the coworkers they leave behind. While this overall shift can be positive, this is an excellent example of possible regret.

This employee left on a negative note, and it is human nature to be focused on the negative effect their leaving had on the team. This is a good example of the **horn effect**—focusing on a minor flaw you can't get past while ignoring all the positive skills and contributions the individual made. Don't let one negative become the basis of your overall evaluation of the employee. This is true when you interview new candidates or assess your current employee's performance.

What should you say if you're called to provide a **reference**? Answer any inquiries honestly. You're likely to be asked questions about the specific job duties the individual performed and how well they performed those duties. The caller may also describe the position and job duties for which your former employee is being considered and ask if you think they are capable of performing that job. Your answers should reflect the individual's job performance.

Depending on who is conducting the **reference check**, you may get questions about the individual's dependability and reliability as an employee. If their abrupt termination was the only negative in their record, once again, don't let it overshadow all your remarks. However, it would be appropriate to mention it.

Take the lead from the caller and answer any questions honestly. If there is negative information to share, do so with diplomacy and grace.

CLOSING THOUGHTS

Ensuring graceful endings is one of the most difficult tasks you will have as a manager. You are dealing with people's lives, and that makes this process complicated and very human. However, ending employment relationships is an integral part of business. You always want to take it seriously, and hopefully this section has provided some guidance on getting through it in the best possible way.

GLOSSARY OF
PEOPLE MANAGEMENT TERMS

Accident: An undesired event that results in physical harm to a person or damage to property.

Active Listening: The communication technique that requires the listener to fully concentrate, understand, and respond to the speaker to ensure that messages are being related completely and properly.

Affirmative Action: The practice in which employers identify conspicuous imbalances in their workforce and take positive steps to correct underrepresentation of protected classes.

Age Discrimination in Employment Act (ADEA): The federal law that prohibits discrimination in employment for persons age forty and over except where age is a bona fide occupational qualification.

Alternative Staffing: The use of alternative recruiting sources and workers who are not regular employees; also known as **Flexible Staffing**.

Americans with Disabilities Act (ADA): The act that prohibits discrimination against a qualified individual with a disability because of the disability of such individual.

Attorney-Client Privilege: A legal privilege used to protect communications between an attorney and the client. The privilege can be used when legal advice is sought from an attorney acting in that capacity, when the primary purpose for the request is for legal advice rather than business advice, and provided all communication is kept confidential between the attorney and the client.

Base Pay: The basic compensation an employee receives, usually as a wage or salary.

Behavioral Interview: A type of interview that focuses on how an applicant previously handled real work situations.

Bias: The result that occurs when an individual's values, beliefs, prejudices, or preconceived notions distort their decisions and actions.

BIPOC: The acronym meaning Black, Indigenous or other people of color; also known as **protected classes**.

Boomerang Employees: A worker who quits their current position with an employer and then wants to come back at a later time.

Candidate Experience: The impression an applicant or candidate forms of an organization during the recruiting and hiring process.

Career Development: The process by which an individual progresses through a series of stages in their careers, each of which is characterized by relatively unique issues, themes, and tasks.

Career Planning: Actions and activities that individuals perform in order to give direction to their work life.

Civil Rights Act of 1991: The federal law that expands the possible damage awards available to victims of intentional discrimination to include compensatory and punitive damages; gives plaintiffs in cases of alleged intentional discrimination the right to a jury trial.

Closed-Ended Questions: Questions that can usually be answered with yes or no.

Coaching: On-going meetings between supervisors and employees to discuss the employee's career goals.

Code of Ethics: Principles of conduct within an organization that guide decision-making and behavior; also known as a **Code of Conduct**.

Collective Bargaining: The process by which management and union representatives negotiate the employment conditions for a particular bargaining unit for a designated period of time.

Collective Bargaining Agreement (CBA): An agreement or contract negotiated through collective bargaining process.

Common Law: Dictates that custom and usage have the force of law, even if not specifically found in legislatively enacted, codified, written laws.

Compensation System: The structure an organization puts in place to have an orderly way to pay its employees.

Competencies: The set of behaviors encompassing skills, knowledge, abilities, and personal attributes that are critical to successful work accomplishment; critical success factors needed to perform a given role in an organization.

Compressed Workweek: A work schedule that compresses a full week's work into fewer than five days.

Constructive Confrontation: An intervention strategy that focuses on behavior and performance.

Constructive Discharge: The result that occurs when employer makes working conditions so intolerable that an employee has no choice but to resign.

Counseling: A form of intervention in which the emphasis is on the cause of a problem rather than on job performance.

Critical Thinking: The process of making inferences and judgments about the credibility of messages and information communicated to us.

Crowdsourced Data: Compensation data that employees self-report to websites and platforms where users can anonymously submit and view salaries.

DEI (Diversity, Equity, and Inclusion): Initiatives that organizations implement that go beyond equal employment opportunity efforts to ensure all individuals share in processes, activities, and decision-/policy-making in a way that shares power and accessibility to resources. See also **diversity.**

Developmental Activities: Activities that focus on preparing employees for future responsibilities while increasing their capacity to perform their current jobs.

Direct Compensation: Pay that is received by an employee, including base pay, differential pay, and incentive pay.

Disability: A physical or mental impairment that substantially limits one or more major life activities such as bathing, dressing, and so on.

Disability Benefits: Monthly benefits paid under Social Security to workers (and eligible dependents) younger than the Social Security retirement age if they have a disability.

Disciplinary Action: A corrective action that is taken to address an employee's workplace misbehavior.

Discrimination: In the employment concept, making decisions that are either implicitly or explicitly based on some legal protection covered under a federal or state discrimination law. See also **Protected Class**.

Disparate Impact: The result that occurs when the selection rate for a protected class (protected under nondiscrimination laws) is significantly less than the rate for the class with the highest selection rate; also known as **adverse impact**.

Disparate Treatment: The result that occurs when protected classes are intentionally treated differently from other employees or are evaluated by different standards.

Distributed Workforce: A workforce that is dispersed geographically over a wide area, domestically or internationally.

Diversity: Differences in characteristics of people; can involve personality, work style, race, age, ethnicity, gender, religion, education, functional level at work, and so on.

E-Learning: The delivery of formal and informal training and educational materials, processes, and programs via the use of electronic media.

Emotional Compensation: Seven universal human needs that allow people to thrive at work. They are respect, recognition, belonging, autonomy, personal growth, meaning, and progress.

Emotional Intelligence (EI): The ability of an individual to be sensitive to and understanding of the emotions of others and to manage their own emotions and impulses.

Employee Assistance Programs (EAPs): Company-sponsored programs that deliver a variety of health-related services, which are provided by licensed professionals or organizations and offer employees a high degree of confidentiality.

Employee Referral Program: A program that encourages and rewards current employees to refer candidates to open positions.

Employment Branding: The process of positioning an organization as an "employer of choice" in the labor market.

Employment Offer: The formal process that makes the hiring decision official; should immediately follow the final decision to hire a candidate; formally communicated through offer letter; also known as **job offer.**

Employment-at-Will: The common-law principle stating that employers have the right to hire, fire, demote, and promote whomever they choose for any reason unless there is a law or contract to the contrary and that employees have the right to quit a job at any time.

Employment Testing: Any tool or step used in the employment selection process. Commonly includes written tests, skill demonstration, or other assessment tool.

Equal Employment Opportunity Commission (EEOC): The federal agency responsible for enforcing nondiscrimination laws and handling alleged complaints.

Equal Pay Act (EPA): The federal law that prohibits wage discrimination by requiring equal pay for equal work.

Ergonomics: Design of the work environment to address the physical demands experienced by employees.

Essential Function: A primary job duty that a qualified individual must be able to perform, either with or without accommodation;

a function may be considered essential because it is required in a job or because it is highly specialized.

Ethics: A system of moral principles and values that establish appropriate conduct.

Executive Search Firms: External recruiting method; firms seek out candidates, usually for executive, managerial, or professional positions.

Exempt Employees: Employees who are excluded from the Fair Labor Standards Act overtime pay requirements.

Exit Interviews: Interview conducted when an employee is terminating with a company in which employee is asked to share views on selected issues.

Extrinsic Rewards: Rewards such as pay, benefits, bonuses, promotions, achievement awards, time off, more freedom and autonomy, special assignments, and so on.

Fair Labor Standards Act (FLSA): The federal law that regulates employee overtime status, overtime pay, child labor, minimum wage, record-keeping, and other administrative concerns.

Family and Medical Leave Act (FMLA): The federal law that provides employees with up to twelve weeks of unpaid leave to care for family members or because of a serious health condition of the employee.

Feedback: Input that a manager provides an employee regarding their job performance.

First-Impression Error: A type of interviewer bias in which an interviewer makes snap judgments and lets first impressions (either positive or negative) cloud the interview.

Flextime: A work schedule that requires employees to work an established number of hours per week but allows starting and ending times to vary.

Gamification: The application of typical elements of game playing used as an approach of engaging learners.

Generation X: The group of people born roughly between the years of 1965 and 1980.

Generation Z: The group of people born roughly between 1997 and 2014.

Goal: A clear statement, usually in one sentence, of the purpose and intent of a department, a project, or a program.

Group Interview: A type of interview in which multiple job candidates are interviewed by one or more interviewers at the same time or where multiple people in an organization interview a single job candidate.

Halo Effect: A type of interviewer bias in which interviewer allows one strong point in a candidate's favor to overshadow all other information.

Horn Effect: A type of interviewer bias in which the interviewer allows one strong point that works against candidate to overshadow all other information.

Hostile Environment Harassment: The type of harassment that occurs when sexual or other discriminatory conduct is so severe and pervasive that it interferes with an individual's performance; creates an intimidating, threatening, or humiliating work environment; or perpetuates a situation that affects the employee's psychological well-being.

Hybrid Work Arrangement: A work model that combines remote and in-person work and workers.

Implied Contract: Exists when an agreement is implied from circumstances even though there is no express agreement between employer and employee.

Incentive Pay: A form of direct compensation in which employers pay for performance beyond normal expectations to motivate employees to perform at higher levels.

Independent Contractor: Workers who are not covered by FLSA regulations as determined by the IRS 20-Factor Test.

Indirect Compensation: A form of compensation commonly referred to as benefits.

Individual Development Plan: A tool to assist employees in their career development. Its primary purpose is to help them reach short- and long-term career goals and to improve current job performance.

Internal Equity: The result that occurs when people feel that performance or job differences result in corresponding differences in pay rates.

Intrinsic Rewards: Meaningful work, good feedback on performance, autonomy, and other factors that lead to high levels of satisfaction in the job.

Investigation: A detailed search for facts involving records, witness interviews, and other inputs.

Involuntary Termination: The type of termination that occurs when employers discharge particular employees for cause (e.g., poor performance or violations of employer policy).

Job Analysis: The systematic study of jobs to determine what activities and responsibilities they include, relative importance and relationship with other jobs, personal qualifications necessary for performance of jobs, and conditions under which work is performed.

Job Burnout: The depletion of physical/mental resources caused by excessive striving to reach an unrealistic work-related goal.

Job Description: A summary of the most important features of a job, including required tasks, knowledge, skills, abilities, responsibilities, and reporting structure.

Job Postings: These can be an **internal recruiting method** that allows current employees the chance to respond to announcements of positions. When used externally to recruit candidates for current positions, they are also referred to as **job listings**.

Job Satisfaction: The extent to which an employee feels content and self-motivated in their job, especially when they know that their work adds value.

Job Sharing Programs: Programs that allow two or more employees to work part time in the same job to create the full-time equivalent.

Knowledge: One's level of learning characterized by ability to recall specific facts.

Layoffs: A type of involuntary termination that is usually the result of a change in business conditions. Also referred to as a **reduction in force.**

Leadership: The ability of an individual to influence a group or another individual toward the achievement of goals and results.

Learning Organization: An organization characterized by a capability to adapt to changes in environment.

Learning Styles: Ways individuals learn and process ideas.

Leaves of Absence: Periods of time away from work that an employer grants to an employee for a variety of reasons.

Lifelong Learning: The ongoing pursuit of knowledge for either personal or professional gain.

Mediation: The method of nonbinding dispute resolution involving a third party who helps disputing parties reach a mutually agreeable decision.

Mentoring: A developmentally oriented relationship between two individuals.

Merit Pay: A situation in which an individual's performance is the basis for either the amount or timing of pay increases; also called performance-based pay.

Microaggressions: Indirect, subtle, or unintentional interactions or behavior that communicate bias or discrimination against members of a protected class. They can include looks, gestures, inflections, or body language.

Microlearning: An approach to learning that delivers quick modules of three to ten minutes that can be delivered just in time.

Millennials: The group of people born roughly between the years 1981 and 1997. Also known as Generation Y.

Mission Statement: A statement that specifies what the company does, who its customers are, and the priorities it has set in pursuing its work.

Mobile Technology: Technology that is portable and designed for use on mobile computing devices such as smartphones and tablets.

Mobile Recruiting: The use of mobile technology for the recruiting of candidates.

Motivation: Factors that initiate, direct, and sustain human behavior over time.

National Labor Relations Act (NLRA): The federal law that protects the rights of employees to organize unhampered by management; also known as the **Wagner Act.**

National Labor Relations Board (NLRB): The federal agency that has authority to conduct union representation elections and investigate unfair labor practices.

Needs Assessment: A process by which an organization's needs are identified in order to help the organization accomplish its objectives.

Negligent Hiring: The hiring of an employee who the employer knew or should have known, based on a reasonable pre-hire investigation of the employee's background, posed a risk to others in the workplace.

Negligent Retention: The retention of employees who engage in misconduct both during and after working hours.

Nonexempt Employees: Employees covered under FLSA regulations, including overtime pay requirements.

Occupational Illness: A medical condition or disorder, other than one resulting from an occupational injury, caused by exposure to environmental factors associated with employment.

Occupational Injury: An injury that results from a work-related accident or exposure involving a single incident in the work environment.

Occupational Safety and Health Act (OSHA): The federal law that established the first national policy for safety and health and continues to deliver standards that employers must meet to guarantee the health and safety of their employees.

Occupational Safety and Health Administration (OSHA): The federal agency that administers and enforces the Occupational Safety and Health Act of 1970.

Offer Letter: A document that formally communicates the employment offer, making the hiring decision official.

Older Workers Benefit Protection Act (OWBPA): The federal law that amended the Age Discrimination in Employment Act to include all employee benefits; also provided terminated employees with time to consider group termination or retirement programs and consult an attorney.

Onboarding: The process of new employee integration into the organization; often lasts up to six months or a year.

On-the-Job Training (OJT): The training provided to employees at the work site utilizing demonstration and performance of job tasks to be accomplished.

Open-Ended Question: A question that can't be answered with a yes or no (for example, "Tell me about how you . . .").

Organizational Culture: Shared attitudes and perceptions in an organization.

Organizational Development (OD): The process of enhancing the effectiveness of an organization and the well-being of its members through planned interventions.

Organizational Exit: The process of managing the way people leave an organization.

Organizational Learning: Certain types of learning activities or processes that may occur at any one of several levels in an organization.

Orientation: The initial phase of employee training that covers job responsibilities and procedures, organizational goals and strategies, and company policies.

Outplacement: A systematic process by which a laid-off or terminated employee is counseled in the techniques of career self-appraisal and in securing a new job that is appropriate to their talents and needs.

Outsourcing: A flexible staffing option in which an independent company with a specialized operating function will contract with a company to assume full operational responsibility for the function.

Overtime Pay: The required pay for nonexempt workers under FLSA at one-and-a-half times the regular rate of pay for hours worked over forty hours in a workweek.

Panel Interview: A type of interview in which structured questions are spread across a group; the individual who is most competent in the relevant area usually asks the question.

Pay Equity: The practice of identifying and addressing pay gaps to ensure that they are not the result of bias or discrimination. Also known as **Salary Equity.**

Pay Transparency: The practice of allowing compensation information such as salary ranges or employees' pay figures to be visible to others either internally, externally, or a combination of both. Also known as **Compensation Transparency.**

Performance Appraisal: A process that measures the degree to which an employee accomplishes work requirements.

Performance Evaluation: Process that measures the degree to which an employee accomplishes work requirements.

Performance Improvement Plan: A written plan that provides an underperforming employee the details of performance deficiencies and the performance results required by a specified date.

Performance Management: The process of maintaining or improving employee job performance through the use of performance assessment tools, coaching, and counseling as well as providing continuous feedback.

Performance Standards: Expectations of management translated into behaviors and results that employees can deliver.

Policy: A broad statement that reflects an organization's philosophy, objectives, or standards concerning a particular set of management or employee activities.

Prescreening Interview: A type of interview that is useful when an organization has a high volume of applicants for a job and face-to-face interviews are needed to judge prequalification factors.

Progressive Discipline: A system of increasingly severe penalties for employee discipline.

Protected Class: People who are covered under a federal or state discrimination law; groups protected by EEO designations include women, African-Americans, Hispanics, Native Americans, Asian-Americans, people age forty or older, the disabled, veterans, and religious groups.

Quid Pro Quo Harassment: A type of sexual harassment that occurs when an employee is forced to choose between giving in to a superior's sexual demands and forfeiting an economic benefit such as a pay increase, a promotion, or continued employment.

Reasonable Accommodation: Modifying the job application process, work environment, or circumstances under which a job is performed to enable a qualified individual with a disability to be considered for the job and perform its essential functions.

Regulation: A rule or order issued by a government agency; often has the force of law.

Reliability: Ability of an instrument to measure consistently.

Remote Workers: Traditionally known as telecommuters, individuals who work from home or other location either permanently or intermittently.

Reskilling: The practice of providing current employees skills for a new position or retraining them in the skills needed for a changing business climate.

Resume: A document prepared by job candidate (or a professional hired by a candidate) to highlight a candidate's strengths and experience.

Retaliatory Discharge: A result of an employer punishing an employee for engaging in activities protected by the law (e.g., filing a discrimination charge or opposing unlawful employer practices).

Retention: The ability to keep talented employees in an organization.

Reverse Mentoring: The practice of pairing older workers with younger ones so they can educate each other (rather than the mentor always being the older worker).

Risk Management: The use of insurance and other strategies in an effort to prevent or minimize an organization's exposure to liability in the event a loss or injury occurs.

Safety: Freedom from hazard, risk, or injury.

Salary: A uniform amount of money paid to a worker regardless of how many hours are worked.

Salary Localization: A pay strategy that is based on the cost of living and/or the cost of labor in a particular geographic location. Also known as **pay localization**.

Salary Portability: A compensation method used to determine an employee's salary when the employee moves to a location where no benchmark for compensation has been set up. The local pay rate is combined with compensation survey data and the employer's own internal benchmarks for a given role to determine how employees should be paid in the location.

Salary Range: In a salary or pay structure, grades set the upper and lower bounds of possible compensation for individuals whose jobs fall in a salary grade.

Security: Physical/procedural measures used to protect people, property, and information in the workplace.

Selection: The process of hiring the most suitable candidate for a vacant position.

Selection Interview: An interview designed to probe areas of interest to interviewer in order to determine how well a job candidate meets the needs of the organization.

Seniority: A system that shows preference to employees with the longest service.

Serious Health Condition: As defined in the FMLA, a condition that requires inpatient hospital, hospice, or residential care or continuing physician care.

Sexual Harassment: Unwelcome sexual advances, requests for sexual favors, and other verbal or physical conduct of a sexual nature.

Short-Term Disability (STD) Coverage: Coverage that replaces a portion of lost income for a specified period of time for employees who are ill or have nonwork-related injuries.

Short-Term Objectives: Milestones that must be achieved, usually within six months to one year, in order to reach long-term objectives.

Sick Leave: A specified period of time during which employees who are ill or have non-work-related injuries receive their full salary.

Staffing: The function that identifies organizational human capital needs and attempts to provide an adequate supply of qualified individuals for jobs in an organization.

Standards: For an operations department, the yardstick by which the amount and quality of output are measured.

Stay Interviews: A one-on-one conversation with an employee that helps employers understand what might make an employee leave or stay before they even consider hopping to another job.

Stereotyping: The type of interviewer bias that involves forming generalized opinions about how people of a given gender, religion, or race appear, think, act, feel, or respond.

Strategic Management: Processes and activities used to formulate business objectives, practices, and policies.

Strategic Planning: The art and science of formulating, developing, implementing, and evaluating cross-functional decisions that enable an organization to achieve its objectives.

Strategic Thinking: The process in which people think about, assess, view, and create the future for themselves and others.

Strategies: The methods that provide the direction that enables an organization to achieve its long-term objectives.

Stress: A mental and physical condition that results from a real or perceived threat and the inability to remove it or cope with it.

Stress Interview: A type of interview in which the interviewer assumes an aggressive posture to see how a candidate responds to stressful situations.

Structured Interview: A type of interview in which interviewer asks every applicant the same questions.

Succession Planning: The process of systematically identifying, assessing, and developing leadership talent.

Talent Management: Systems designed to develop processes for attracting, developing, retaining, and utilizing people with the required skills and aptitude to meet current and future business needs.

Tangible Rewards: Non-cash rewards that have monetary value, like gift cards, travel vouchers, and merchandise given to an employee to recognize and thank them for a job well done.

Targeted Interview: A type of interview in which interviewer asks each applicant questions that are from the same knowledge, skill, or ability area; also called a **Patterned Interview.**

Team Interview: A type of interview used in situations in which the position relies heavily on team cooperation; supervisors, subordinates, and peers are usually part of the process.

Title VII of the Civil Rights Act of 1964: The federal law that prohibits discrimination or segregation based on race, color, national origin, religion, and gender in all terms and conditions of employment.

Total Rewards: All forms of financial returns that employees receive from their employers.

Training: The process of providing knowledge, skills, and abilities (KSAs) specific to a task or job.

Turnover: An annualized formula that tracks number of separations and total number of workforce employees for each month.

Unfair Labor Practice (ULP): A violation of statutory right (of the employee and the employer) under labor-relations statutes.

Examples of employer ULPs: interfering with employees exercising their rights and retaliating or discriminating against those who do, and refusing to bargain in good faith. Examples of labor unions ULP: coercing employees and discriminating against employees who choose not to join the union, unfair representation, excessive membership fees, and refusing to bargain in good faith.

Union: Formal association of employees that promotes the interests of its membership through collective action.

Upskilling: Similar to reskilling, the practice of providing current employees skills needed in existing positions.

Validity: Ability of an instrument to measure what it is intended to measure.

Values: A set of principles that describes what is important to an organization, dictates employee behavior, and creates the organization's culture.

Vesting: The process by which a retirement benefit becomes nonforfeitable.

Vicarious Liability: The legal doctrine under which a party can be held liable for the wrongful actions of another party.

Vision Statement: A vivid, guiding image of an organization's desired future.

Wellness Programs: Preventive health programs offered by employers designed to improve the health and physical well-being of employees both on and off the job.

Whistleblowers: A person or an employee who discloses information or activity of wrongdoing about an organization.

Workers Compensation: The state insurance program designed to protect workers in cases of work-related injuries or diseases related to workers' employment.

Workforce Planning: The process an organization uses to analyze its current base of employees and determine steps it must take to prepare for future skill and labor needs.

Work-Related Disability: A physical condition (accident or illness) that is caused, aggravated, precipitated, or accelerated by work activity or the work environment.

Workweek: Any fixed, recurring period of 168 hours (7 days x 24 hours = 168 hours).

INDEX

ABOUT THE AUTHORS

A writing partnership was born when the first edition of *The Big Book of HR* hit the market in 2012. Drawing on their collective experience, Barbara Mitchell and Cornelia Gamlem wrote the book because managing people is the most challenging part of any leader's day. Since then, they've gone on to write four more books and collaborate on a weekly blog.

Both authors are influencers to the business and HR communities. They have been interviewed in major radio markets around the country, been quoted in major publications, contributed to online media, been featured on podcasts, and are frequent speakers to business groups. Among their writing awards, they are most proud of the recognition they received from The Next Generation Indie Book Awards, the largest International Book Awards for Indie Authors and Publishers; namely, 2020 Award Winner for *The Manager's Answer Book*, and 2022 Finalist for *The Big Book of HR, 10th Anniversary Edition*.

Cornelia and Barbara bring a wealth of business experience and knowledge to their writing partnership. They were both HR leaders in major corporations before they started their individual consulting practices where they each worked with a wide variety of businesses and organizations.

Cornelia Gamlem is passionate about helping organizations develop and maintain respectful workplaces.

She's been active with national employers' groups focused on workplace equity and diversity and has served on task forces that influenced public policy, testified before the Equal Employment Opportunity Commission on several occasions, and also served in national leadership volunteer roles with The Society for Human Resource Management.

Education has also played a key role. Cornelia holds a master's degree in Human Resource Management from Marymount University and an undergraduate degree in Business Administration from California State University, Sacramento. She achieved Life Certification as Senior Professional in Human Resources (SPHR) from the Human Resource Certification Institute (HRCI).

Giving back is important, and Cornelia has been an instructor at a number of colleges in the Washington DC metro area and a technical editor for McGraw Hill Education. She currently serves on the board of directors of SouthWest Writers in Albuquerque, New Mexico where she currently lives and writes.

Barbara Mitchell believes that finding, hiring, engaging, and retaining the best talent available is critical to organizations.

She gained a strong business foundation working in finance, marketing, and operations before entering the HR profession. Education also played a role. Barbara has a degree from North Park University, Chicago, Illinois, and has taken graduate-level business courses at UCLA, the University of Denver, and Loyola Marymount University, Los Angeles.

Being active in the communities in which she lives and works is important to Barbara. She has served on the board of directors of national (the Employment Management Association) and local human resource organizations. In the broader community, she has served as a board member of The National Presbyterian Church, the Northern Virginia Habitat for Humanity affiliate, and the Loudoun County Literacy Council. She supports the Smithsonian's American Art Museum as a video docent in Washington, DC where she currently lives and writes.

STAY CONNECTED WITH
CORNELIA & BARBARA

Visit our website: *www.bigbookofhr.com*
Read our weekly blog: *www.bigbookofhr.com/blog*

Connect on LinkedIn
- **Cornelia:** *https://www.linkedin.com/in/corneliagamlem/*
- **Barbara:** *https://www.linkedin.com/in/mitchellbarbara/*

Follow us on Twitter: @bigbookofhr